MW00425700

A
Memoir

Growing Up at Mooseheart

A Memoir

John DelMonaco

SIMPLY
ECLECTIC
BOOKS

Growing Up At Mooseheart – A Memoir
John DelMonaco

ISBN: 978-1-939288-20-2
Library of Congress Control Number: 2013941847

ALL RIGHTS RESERVED
©2013 Georgia Candoli

No part of this publication may be translated, reproduced or transmitted in any form without prior permission in writing from the publisher. Publisher and editor are not liable for any typographical errors, content mistakes, inaccuracies, or omissions related to the information in this book.

SIMPLY
ECLECTIC
BOOKS

Published by
Simply Eclectic Books, A Wyatt-MacKenzie Imprint
simplyeclecticbooks@wyattmackenzie.com

Printed in the U.S.A.

Acknowledgments

The author recognizes all the hundreds of kids who became his brothers, sisters, and all the parents who became his mothers, and fathers, while at Mooseheart. Grateful thanks are given to the thousands of Moose Lodges and their membership who have supported, and still support, Mooseheart.

Special Remembrances

Evelyn Suzanne Love for giving spiritual insight; Ruth, for a week at the lake where words flowed freely; Ken & Sue, for research; Brother George & Shep, for an atmosphere conducive to rich thoughts and provoking self-realization; Georgia, who inspired the desire to write and always stayed in my heart; Michael, Bette, Denise . . it all started when we were all very young and together.

∾

CONTENTS

Introduction
1979

For the reader unacquainted with any system of care for children, especially orphanages that care for hundreds of children at one time, it is necessary to understand the background against which this story is told.

This brief overview of Mooseheart acquaints the reader with the institution's basic precepts whereby he may more fully relate and appreciate the magnitude of influence this Child City has on the life of the young child during his most formative years.

All children in Mooseheart are orphans. The entrance fee is very high. . . every child has lost one or both of his parents before being eligible for admittance.

A Moose member contributes to his Moose Lodge through his membership dues, part of which go directly to support the Child City of Mooseheart, the family protection plan for all members of the lodge. All children under the age of 14 are eligible for placement in Mooseheart with no further financial obligations whatsoever on the part of the family. A few children were born at Mooseheart and were reared under its auspices a full 18 years through graduation.

The situations are typical of the daily life, the circumstances basically the same for boys and girls alike. The reader will soon learn it is not the situation itself alone, but the method, the value structure, that entwines the child's life as he unfolds into his uniqueness.

There is conflict in this story . . . it rests within the child, in the realm of the unknown. There is expectancy, but it is not known how, why or when events will happen. It is not resolved until the child has lived and experienced actual life.

Mooseheart is the only city in the world devoted entirely to the care of children. Its large, beautiful, 1,100 acre estate; 313 acres devoted to campus and parks, the lake covers 23 acres of water, over two hundred buildings . . . 50 student residences, 5 vocational buildings, its own schools, farms, gardens, gym, House of God, hospital, sports areas, department store, market, post office, power plant, an almost self-sustaining child city.

The school is based on the creed: NO MAN STANDS SO TALL AS WHEN HE STOOPS TO PICK-UP A CHILD.

Since its inception, over 7,000 children have been raised, educated and carefully nurtured within the system.

Mooseheart is the realization of an ideal conceived by its founder, James J. Davis. Sensitive to the stark tragedy and destitution in the lives of so many children, he saw the need for a community in which orphaned children could enjoy all the advantages of a good home, the finest training and the best preparation for life in which the family unit could be preserved as closely as possible. With humble beginnings, he started as an "iron puddler." He was born October 27, 1873 and became the 247th member of the Loyal Order of Moose on October 27, 1906. This date, October 27, is celebrated as 'Mooseheart Day.'

On January 1, 1913, 400,000 members of the Lodge

contributed 25 cents each to build and equip a new home and school for the orphaned children of its members. The name 'Mooseheart' was agreed upon and on July 13, 1913, ground was broken for their dream, 'The Child City of Mooseheart.'

The loss of the male parent is traumatic to the family. What does the surviving wife with children do when this tragedy occurs?

Upon the death of my father, my mother visited Mooseheart to determine our possible placement there. She was 28 years old, her five children ranged from 18 months old to $7^1/2$ years of age. She consented to our entrance and the burden was lifted from her shoulders.

We stayed at Mooseheart for a total of 76 years between the six of us.

My transition from life 'outside' Mooseheart to 'inside' was instant. Once inside the gate I was part of the institution. Everything that was to happen to me from this day forward was for my own well being. I no longer had any way to compare.

Health care started the day of entrance and was carefully observed every day thereafter. Health, however, is physical, mental, social and spiritual.

The Mooseheart Health Care Center was the most modern, up-to-date facility that can be provided. The medical staff consisted of a physician and surgeon; an ear, nose and throat specialist, an eye specialist, dentist, orthodontist, nurses and a full staff of technicians.

The Child Guidance Clinic rendered a service to every child through a thorough testing program for best placement in the home, school and vocational pursuits. Special abilities and achievements were carefully considered and used to prepare the student for his future. Disabilities, personality characteristics and emotional life, along with speech and achievement levels, serve to give a complete picture for proper care as an individual. The purpose is to give as complete knowledge of each individual child as possible.

Mooseheart participated in many scientific studies as a controlled source for research in health and psychological analyses. Very few situations exist where children can be so closely observed over a long, controlled period of years.

The rules and regulations of Mooseheart were based on the results of this research. Mooseheart was the outstanding example in the study of normalcy of children.

This story may seem to tell the life of a child who is free of all outward conflicts. It is difficult to understand, but on the whole, this was so. There was no direct need for rebellion for the purpose of the institution was to blend the lives of hundreds of diverse persons and personalities into one cohesive unit. Critics may offer all sorts of criticism, however, I ask; if you were given 1,200 children and knew not how many more were coming to your arms, how best would you manage?

Training began in the Baby Village where the aim is to develop desirable physical, mental and emotional attitudes, teach children to get along with others, to observe the rights of the group, and to have a proper respect for authority. It extends to the day of graduation.

We learned discipline, order and sharing through routines. Particular stress is laid upon good habit formation. Responsibility is best learned by doing the job yourself.

Children learned to put away their clothes and personal belongings when in Baby Village. By seven years of age they could do most household chores. By nine they are skilled in all household duties and can do them to the last day of graduation. A three-story house can be cleaned in a few hours and sparkle as though 30 children never lived there. The routines save tempers. The assignment list discouraged arguments. We may have griped about doing the work but we didn't feel abused because we had to do it.

Early influences during impressionable youth are often indelible for life. The routines gave security, a sense of belonging, of finding one's own space. I learned to accept it and flourished in the acceptances.

We had no television. Listening to the radio sharpened our imagination, it brought in the outside world and we tuned ourselves to the characteristics of our heroes.

In the early years of Mooseheart, children received clothes through the requisition system. We learned to save money but were unskilled in the purchasing of our needs. Frequent visits and trips off-campus allowed an easy adjustment to the work-a-day world.

Children were free to roam the campus within specific limitations. There are quiet moments away from sounds of civilization that allow for introspection, a surfacing of the inner person. The lake, farm, the open grounds, offer time and beauty to be alone, to become acquainted and to like ourselves a little more. It was our home.

Mooseheart had a full educational program, kindergarten through 12th grade. The school is a member of the North Central Association of Secondary Schools and Colleges and is supervised by the Department of Public Instruction of the State of Illinois. Most unique is the requirement that each child must learn a trade in preparation for his life's work. Many students qualify for scholarships; graduates are scientists, authors, professionals, as well as skilled workers.

Quality, the expectation of excellence, was the standard set in all we did. Mediocrity and permissiveness were not part of our life. I've never known any child to accept less than his best once he has achieved the pride of being proud. The school soon became known as the school of champions; in music, sports, vocational creativity and high academic achievement.

Teachers are very influential as they are the direct link to the quality of expectations of the outside world. We learned to accept our teachers as we did our matrons and others in charge of us. They soon became vital in our lives and were part of the Mooseheart family. Learning to live with one another was basic to the concept of Mooseheart. We strove to accomplish. We received values and desires, as well as books and homework.

Life was a growing up to be the most fulfilling we can be. We learned to be appreciative, to trust those whom we valued and emulated.

Much emphasis was on sports with varsity football, basketball, track, and wrestling. In addition, the intramural program was offered in conjunction with a standard physical educational program for all ages during the entire 12-month period.

We were programmed to experience; exposed to classical sounds, sculpture, poetry, theatre . . . always encouraged to participate. To do was important. Participation meant growing socially, emotionally and personally. The artistic program in Mooseheart was varied and most of the students were involved in one program or another. At one time, 1,000 of the 1,500 children were members of the Music Department. Each Sunday of the year a program was presented on the stage, everyone had to attend. The band, orchestra, and dance band gave concerts. There were solo organ and piano recitals. Solos and ensembles prepared for the festivals, operettas, oratorios, plays, skits, etc. Some children were in so many organizations they appeared on the stage 52 Sundays a year. Opportunities for participation and leadership were omnipresent.

An edict basic to Mooseheart is: EVERY CHILD SHALL RECEIVE AN ACADEMIC EDUCATION, LEARN A TRADE, USE HIS HANDS AND BRAIN, BE SENSITIVE IN HIS HEART.

Growing up often means enjoying places and doing activities by yourself, or with a friend with no adults present. We were free of manufactured toys, could wander and wonder. We had over 300 acres containing a lake full of fish, a dump full of good junk, a nursery full of rabbits and birds, the farm and barn with the cows, pigs, chickens and lots of open fields to run and chase one another.

Nature was bountiful and provided nuts for cracking, snow for sledding, ice for skating, stones for slingshots. With nothing to do all day we found ourselves so busy we hated to return to the halls for dinner.

One of the basic precepts of the sponsoring Moose Lodges is: THOU SHALT BELIEVE IN GOD, AND WORSHIP HIM AS THY CONSCIENCE DICTATES.

Belief in a supreme power has always been a part of our life. Religious guidance has a profound influence in building character and is totally supported by Mooseheart. Many students have become priests, ministers. The faith each student practiced when young has provided a basic foundation, not only for his family, but also for the good of society. To have faith is to know there is a knowing.

All students at Mooseheart attended church services every Sunday and were trained in the faith, which prevailed in the original home. One class period each week is set aside for religious instruction and is taught by the Catholic and Protestant chaplains. Bible study was held for 15 minutes every evening on school days.

All mothers, who choose, came to Mooseheart to stay with their children. One of the blessings of Mooseheart is the fact housemothers are usually mothers themselves. Their innate desire to give to children is somehow miraculously spread over all those in her charge even though they are not her natural children.

None of our family ever knew the agony and inner stress this one decision must have caused our mother, "Should I place my children in Mooseheart? Should I go myself?"

Each day she was present at Mooseheart brought a deeper faith that her children were better off than had they stayed in the city. Mother no longer questioned if it would have been possible for her to work and to give the wealth of care, attention, schooling and quality of life her children were receiving. The blessing was evident in each and every day.

The combination of religious training, many activities and organizations, a strict routine schedule and discipline, offered freedom to associate with the opposite sex in a casual get-acquainted matter. We could appreciate each other as individuals. As we grew, the normal desires expressed themselves and we then respected each other from an acquaintance of knowing on a long-term basis.

Home life was separated into a boys and girls campus. Each campus had definite known boundaries, separated by a sidewalk, road or other unfenced indications. The entire campus was without fences except for the farm animal areas. School life and activities were mixed and functioned as any normal life situation.

Living and loving your home made leaving extremely difficult. How does an orphan feel when he has to leave the only home he has ever known, one he has learned to love and respect? The people who were first strangers are now his mothers, fathers, sisters and brothers. I was actually leaving two families, a mother and four brothers, plus, the 1,200 other kids I lived and associated with each and every day.

We children were prepared as best can be in head and heart for the outside world, but, sometimes not for the finality of actually leaving. As must be faced by every child, he must leave alone.

∾

The Death of My Father

My father died when I was seven years old; actually he didn't die, he was killed in an automobile accident. I remember riding in a car with my aunt and as we crossed a street she pointed to a corner apartment building and said, "There's where your Dad was killed. He was coming home late one night and some guy ran the red light, knocked his car so hard it rolled over and went right into the bottom floor." I looked briefly. The window was clear; unbroken and looked just like all the other windows. It was difficult for me to see what she was talking about.

I do remember the car. It was in our back yard; smashed, the roof flat, windows out and easy to crawl into, which I did. I remarked to someone, "The clock is still ticking." I don't recall any sad feelings about my being in the car even though my father was killed in the same place in which I was now sitting. I played around the car, nobody bothered me; to me it was a place to investigate and had its usual fascination as something different to do. It had no personal relationship to me.

My Mom was seated on the big porch swing, my aunts next to her. There was much talking, crying and many people moving around. I wasn't aware that my father was in his casket and that it was in our living room.

The total impact of my father's death did not seem to have reached me. I didn't understand what it was. My Mom had me kneel beside his casket, the lid being open, and I looked at him knowing he was my father. His hands were folded and he appeared just like he always did, my Dad. We said prayers at the prompting of my mother. I distinctly remember the Lord's Prayer. We knelt by the casket for a long time. I was very quiet. Mom said, "Kiss your father, John." I leaned over and put my lips on his. I looked at him a long while, my mind fixing this image into my memory forever.

Time meant very little to me. I was offered candy, if I would stay home from the funeral. I accepted it and ate it. I then recall running through the doorway and jumping off the stairs and squeezing my way into a car. It was a long drive to wherever we were going. It was hot.

When the car came to a stop we were in a place that had all kinds of statues, trees, and small brick-like stones on the ground. People were getting out of cars and moved to a large hill of dirt where my Mother stood. I looked and saw the same casket that was in our house. Everyone was circled around it. I noticed the wide cloth like bands that slowly moved as the casket was lowered into the ground. Others started dropping dirt on top of it; I did the same. Someone took my hand and as I looked back I could see the casket deep in the ground, covered with flowers and dirt. I don't recall ever thinking my father was inside it.

My memories of my Dad are few . . . boating in a park, where I almost fell in trying to sail a sailboat; working in his garage and sitting in a pan of some fluid scrubbing parts of motors; seeing him once in the raised bed platform, very quiet and asleep. Mom said, "He had his teeth pulled, be quiet." Another incident involved one of my brothers flying through the air and landing on the bed, crying, with the sound of my Dad's voice coming through very angry.

Very seldom, if ever, can I picture sitting at the table eating with my four brothers. I do remember adults being present, but no awareness of a family feeling. Only once do I recall taking one of my younger brothers to school for the first time and my own personal awareness of myself as being in school. This always seemed strange to me.

Our house was right along the streetcar tracks, the elevated streetcars above, and the fire station across the street. My brothers and I used to wake-up early in the morning holding the blanket in front of us, bouncing on the bed and covering our heads so people in the streetcar wouldn't see us. The front house had a yard and next to the sidewalk was some sort of food stand that sold food to passersby. I think it belonged to my family; I'm not sure.

I once had the measles and remember the shades always being closed. The belly-stove was next to my room and was always flashing colors through the Isinglass window.

The basement was large and had a coal bin at one end that received coal from a hole in the sidewalk by means of a chute. 1 played in there many times. Also, there was a wine room; large wooden barrels were up off the floor in two rows on each side. I once went from barrel-spigot to spigot sucking the dripping wine until they found me asleep on the floor. Why they took grapes and crushed them in laundry rollers I never did know. All I remember was the talking, talking, talking and hands moving very quickly; grape boxes filled the basement from floor to ceiling.

I had never thought of it before, but I did not know if this was our house or if we were living with someone else; there were just so many people around all the time, it was hard to tell.

I remember at Halloween being dressed as a ghost. I recall being at my godfather's house, playing "keep it away" with a small doll, throwing it through the air and suddenly finding myself in the bath tub, blood flowing from the back of my head. The doctor's place was up two flights of back stairs and I soon had my head stitched.

Most of the incidents of my early life that I remember are very few, until Mooseheart. They barely stand out separately from the rest of my life. They are very vague and as hazy as the state when one awakens slowly from sleep, opening his eyes, mistily seeing something and then dropping back into slumber once again.

The first positive sense of my life and total awareness of my surroundings was when I heard the steam whistle blow as we entered Mooseheart.

THE FIRST DAY

The date was May 28, a Sunday. Sitting together in an overcrowded car with me, were my four brothers, my mother, one aunt, with Grandpa at the steering wheel. The car entered the campus and soon stopped to allow people to cross the street; the people were only a colorful array of Sunday clothes passing in a short parade. Without warning a steam whistle blew. I opened the door of the car and headed in the direction of the crowd; surely there was a fire to be seen.

Such was the arrival of my family into the lap of Mooseheart. The power plant steam whistle was to regulate my daily life from this day forward, from getting out of bed, going to school, and attendance at concerts to the last lonely sound heard before going to sleep.

The stop at the New York Building was a relief, we all piled out of the car. It was hot, humid and the long drive from the city had baked our skins. Everyone stretched and stood silently, slowly turning, taking in the new surroundings. So many trees, so much grass, the water tower jutting immensely against the sky, the tall gray smoke stack pointing thin veils of white smoke against the blue only to fade into nothingness. Across the open campus grounds, children of all ages headed in the direction of the smoke stack as if being devoured by it. Soon all movement vanished and we stood alone in silence. Mom stood facing Grandpa, tears in her eyes, "Well, Pa, guess we better go in. They'll be waiting for us."

The suitcases were lifted from the trunk, everyone taking a load suitable to his size. The youngest managed only him self, as he was only 18 months. At seven, I was the eldest, and managed a small suitcase. The other three brothers carried Mom's purse, a few paper bags full of clothes and a large brown envelope with details of information regarding the family. We walked down the long, white, concrete sidewalk. We took the first steps into what was to be our new life for the next 12 to 18 years.

The door opened and, the hall matron greeted us.

"Good afternoon, I'm so glad to see you." She extended her hand to Mom and pulled her toward her in a soft, affectionate hug, their cheeks barely touching.

"Welcome to Mooseheart," she said quietly, "You're so welcomed." They stayed close for a while longer, trying to ease the anxiety of the moment.

"Well, kids," said Mom, as she moved toward us, "Let's get settled and maybe we can have a glass of milk." The bags were gathered and everyone started up the stairs.

"Your rooms are ready for you on the second floor," the matron informed us.

The four older kids were in one large room. The 18-month old brother was placed with Mom. We stood in the doorway of our new home. The room was large; a center carpet filled the space between the beds. Clean white sheets, a pillow and a white, knobby cover over the top of the beds made it look like cleanliness and order were part of the expected daily pattern of life. The window framed a picture of tall, green-leafed trees, the sidewalk ribboned into the divided street and ended in a glimpse of a three-story windowed grey brick building. The water tower hovered over pine trees in the background, the other road was lost in its winding, leading to who knows where.

We stood there for a long time. So much room. For each of us a bed of our very own. We seemed to drift naturally to our right places, sat on the beds and looked at one another. The exact feelings of the very young are difficult to recall, you are driven so deeply into yourself that you just feel everything intensely and somehow it all seems to come out in tears. This place was strange, so new, and the future and what would happen to us was unknown. Secretly scared, we felt utter loneliness.

We could hear other voices down the hall, coming closer. Two heads poked around the door, silently looking us over and finally saying, "Hi." It seemed strange to have someone we didn't know enter our room. They seemed happy. I remember vaguely their remarks about 'being here for three weeks, testing, doctor looking them over, shots in the arm and a haircut.'

We had dinner together, at the same table. The other two families who entered a few weeks earlier occupied the rest of the tables. We were asked many questions which Mom answered.

We were happy to be in our own room. So much had happened in this one day. The sound of the steam whistle echoed through the darkened trees and softly howled in our room. Mom kissed us all goodnight. The clean sheet smelled of a new world, the knobby covers served to satisfy my fingers for a long time as my mind wondered and wandered. What would happen to us?

For the first time I could remember there were no outside noises, no streetcar traffic. The sounds of the night were soft, the street lamp reflected on the ceiling and the curtain moved easily with the cool, evening breeze. I looked at the lumps that were my brothers in the other beds, one of them was crying softly. Tears filled my eyes and in the diffusion I faded into sleep.

∾

DETENTION HALL

New York Hall served as the reception and detention building for new arrivals to Mooseheart. We stayed there for a few weeks. Little by little we roamed outside on the front lawn, took long walks with Mom and began to "feel at home." One morning we all walked to the barbershop. In twenty minutes, five haircuts were given. A thorough scrutiny of my head by the barber was dismissed with, "Can't find anything here." My head had such a bald feeling that the air felt cold.

I was taken to the hospital almost every day. After I had stripped to my underwear and sat shivering on the couch the doctor finally came in. As the thermometer wavered in my mouth, the doctor turned pages of paper in a folder. Then taking the thermometer from my mouth, he grunted, placed it in a glass and scribbled in the folder.

"Open your mouth" was next with a depressor shoved in. I almost threw up in his hand. He looked under my armpits, tapped my chest, squeezed my belly, and knocked my knees with a rubber hammer.

My toes were pried apart, rubbed with cotton, bent up and down and I yelled because it hurt. He glared at me, went around me and started pounding me on the back and rubbing some small cold, round thing all up and down. My backbone arched as he tested all my bones. I giggled and he laughed, "Ticklish, huh?" and he went at it again.

When I had stepped down from the table, he said, "Now that you're up, take your drawers off." This rather surprised me, what's he going to do? I slowly moved in reply. After making me bend over, having me cough and stand on one foot and then the other, he remarked, "You're in good shape, put your drawers on."

Next came the eyes, his flashlight burning into my head. What was he looking for anyway? "And now the other eye, look up, down, follow my finger with both eyes." Back to the folder, always writing.

Soon a pair of pliers was shoved in my nose and instead of squeezing they spread it apart. "Now your ears." He took a long time looking in them. "Yes, yes, very good." Then he went back to the folder. It seemed like he wrote for an eternity. He mumbled a lot, tapped his pencil on the paper, turned back to other pages and mumbled some more. I got used to the exam but all his mumbling made me feel like there was something wrong and I would be slapped into a hospital bed in a few minutes. My brain must have been so absorbed in this thought that when he turned around so suddenly I jerked back from him and went around the table. He looked at me, smiled and said, "You're in excellent health. Get dressed now and go to the nurse at the desk."

He picked up all the papers and folders and opened the door, stopping and looking back, smiling at me, he said, "Nice to have you with us here at Mooseheart."

I slowly sat down in the chair and stared at the door. He really was nice.

My brother came down the hall holding his arm, crying and awfully unhappy. "What's the matter?" I asked.

"1 got shot," he sobbed as he passed me."

"Shot," I yelled, "What do you mean?" He turned the corner.

I was greeted cheerfully with, "Hello, Hello, Hello," as a nurse circled her friendly arm around my shoulder. Even though she was happy to see me I didn't hear anything she was saying, my eyes were too busy seeing sponges, cotton, empty tubes, rubber hoses, long needles and lots of small jars neatly arranged on a clean towel. My nose snapped open with a strange smell I always associate with hospitals.

She kept blabbing things like, "You're healthy, gotta keep you healthy" and all sorts of other things. All the time my eyes are seeing needles pushed into tubes, bottles punctured, plungers pulled out and stuff filling the glass tube. When the doctor pulled the needle from the bottle and forced the plunger in, the stuff almost hit the ceiling. That was enough for me.

They caught me half way down the hall. The nurse, feeling she was comforting me, buried my head in her bosom. When the doctor released my arm he said, "That's all, son." I looked at my arm; it had a big bump on it. I couldn't understand what my brother was crying about, I didn't even feel it.

As I left the room my arm seemed to swell to twice its size. God, it was beginning to hurt like mad.

Over the years at Mooseheart I visited this same room many times, always to be received joyfully, treated kindly, all the time knowing that I was being taken care of.

There were times, in later years, when all the boys and girls were placed into certain halls under quarantine because of epidemics of chicken pox, whooping cough and the flu. It was one of the rare times I ever saw both young kids and big kids sharing the same hall. At one time 350 kids were in bed during the influenza epidemic.

It wasn't until years later that I understood the early exam, which we all received, not only protected the newcomer but also was a preventive step in stopping the spread of any possible disease throughout the rest of the school.

My other early tangle with the new and mysterious world of medicine came in the form of my first visit to the dentist. Words mean very little to a kid sitting in a dentist's chair for the first time. The experience of having someone slap a piece of wood against your teeth, picking around with metal and scraping your gums is very frightening. I had sucked blood from my finger lots of times but the first taste of it in my mouth convinced me that the dentist had cut my tongue and I was bleeding to death. He shoved a tube in my mouth, filled it with a sweet taste and said, "Spit it out." I did, right on the floor! This got him mad.

"Nurse."

He left the room. The nurse cleaned up the mess. "Next time use the sink there." She pointed to a small round pot-like sink with water in it.

"We'll take you later, clean your teeth and fill one cavity." The napkin was taken from my neck. I was lead out the door. The sun felt good on my back as I walked back to the hall.

The next few days were spent playing and having a good time. Then without forewarning I was taken for a walk in the direction of the hospital. When we passed it I felt relieved. This feeling didn't last long for we were climbing the steps to what was to become known to me as the "Bug House." This place was scary in a different way; everything was just rooms, one after another.

The man who talked to me was hard to understand. I soon found myself busy playing with all sorts of square and round blocks, working color papers, drawing figures, reading black picture blobs, dropping pegs in holes-all sorts of games. It wasn't until many years later that I learned this was a child guidance clinic. The psychological tests were given to determine aptitude, educational development and proper placement in school classes.

Many years later, when I was a teenager, I read the statement; "It is declared, the child, during the period of adolescence, should be guided and not squelched and that the peculiarities and disagreeable traits that the average child exhibits during this period are a part of his development."

I was shifted from hall to hall, one group to another, the reasons unknown to me, but surely well reasoned and planned by those in charge. My freedom had restraints, many permissive activities; hours on Special taught me that too much abuse would give me time for repentance and time to think. There was no corporal punishment. To keep 1,500 kids in line somebody was at the helm, even though we were often ignorant of whom it was.

The Shattering of the Family Unit

The period of time in Detention Hall gradually became very pleasant. We were adjusting to our new home and enjoying the company of our newfound friends. The doctor, dentist and other officials suddenly disappeared from our lives and the days were spent in play.

Then suddenly I was asked to pack my clothes and told I would be moving to North Hope Hall. I shoved all my clothes in a cloth bag and saw my brothers doing the same. The same feeling of fear welled up inside me as the day we first arrived, and along with it the personal concern for what would happen to me.

"Where you going?" I asked my brothers.

They replied, "Wisconsin Hall, Erie Hall." Mom told us later that the two youngest brothers were going to Baby Village.

All that these names meant to me was separation, distance and mystery. I had thought that all of us would be together as a family in the same house here just as we had been before we came to Mooseheart. I was totally and utterly confused.

I threw the bag over my shoulder. As it wobbled on my

back, with the ropes digging into my fingers, I felt only the pain of watching my brothers go one way, me in the opposite direction; my Mother standing with tears in her eyes trying to watch her kids walk away. We were all crying, yet, were assured that everything would be okay because Mother said it would be.

Unknown to each of us was the fact that never again in our lives would we live under the same roof with one another. The only feelings we had were temporary and were ones that left us finally after nights of crying, eating very little and then stuffing ourselves to cover the agony.

Thus took place the shattering of our family unit-from the very dependent and interwoven unit of mother and five sons to the next instant of being alone and orphaned. I did not know at the time what the word orphan meant. My state of mind at that point was locked so deeply within me that words or titles explained nothing.

I was totally unprepared for the next hour or the next week or the next years. I gradually came to know life as an accumulation of buffetings, fights, arguments, defending myself and surviving in the winning of the inner battle within myself. I knew my father but briefly. When I felt the urge to relate to a male figure in my life the agony welled up in tears and ended in the realization that his death not only separated us but also was the reason I was here. I missed him and needed him as part of my life. How much this loss affected my growing up into a man I will never know. I only knew he was gone and the part of me that yearned for the man within the son was empty and wanted to be fulfilled.

Mom came to see me a few days later to check on me,

make sure I was fine and still alive. This joy was short lived. She soon had to leave for Purity Hall. "That's where I'm an assistant matron," she said. I was totally unaware where it was or what she did, she just walked out of my sight.

The loss of my mother became less and less through a "permit" system, which allowed me to see her three times a week for specific assigned hours. The matron wrote the slip, signed it with her name and hour and when I left Mom she signed it and wrote in the time. I don't recall these early visits, other than to see one another and get the hugs, kisses and loving that only a mother can give to her child. The matron hugged me, but the motherly love that flows one into the other seems to be channeled more directly from the natural parent and nourishes her children sufficiently to sustain him for all unseen situations till the next hug and kiss.

Seeing her calmed my anxiety, as I'm sure it did the same for her. Sometimes I would be there when my brothers were there. It was like meeting your best friends. It was not unusual for us not to be together or see each other for weeks . . . unless our permit-time and day were the same.

Over a period of time, the entire hall became brothers and my real brothers were part of the whole. The same happened on the girls campus and everyone in school knew each other and the family was knitted one to the other without regard for name, nationality, creed or any materialistic separation. This was the essential essence of Mooseheart, we became one; in thought, action and belief. There was no other life, we lived together as a self-sustaining organism and we felt we grew healthy and happy as individuals. In later years we were to say, "We know no other way. We loved the end result." Whenever anyone asked, "Where're you from?" we replied, "Mooseheart."

The Artificial Home

North Hope Hall was a big two-story, gray brick building with a large metal two-door opening in the center. The ground in front of the building was covered with small, pebble-like stones. Kids were all over the place, laughing, yelling, and running, all in seemingly unending motion. As I approached the area, remarks came flying through the air at me:

"Hey, here's a new kid." "Where do you come from?" "What hall ya' goin' to be in, huh?" "What's your name, kid?"

"He's D-166, can't you see it on his bag, dummy?"

The big metal door flew open and I was told to turn right. Another pair of large wooden double doors opened and I entered into a huge room, couches, chairs, bookcases, and concrete floor all loomed at me without perspective. I stood frozen. The place was full of kids and I didn't know one of them. My eyes flashed around trying to find a path and only saw everyone staring at me. Mumblings grew louder and finally some kid yelled, "Hey, Mrs. Shuey, here's another new kid."

From around the corner came a small, heavy-set lady, glasses on the end of her nose, smiling and saying words I never heard. My laundry sack was pushed and punched as I passed and finally sent spinning in a circle that threw me off balance. I disappeared down the hall regaining my balance.

The matron was kind, took me into her room, paged through my papers and tried to assure me everything would be just fine.

I briefly recall being shown the locker room and assigned a locker, "This is your very own." The lockers were against both walls and a double row down the center. The large window opened from the far wall by a pull chain and a kid was just going out feet first.

"Jimmy, how many times do I have to tell you not to go out the window? Now you get in here and take a seat in the living room. It's almost time for supper." She grabbed the kid, slapped him on the bottom and led him down the hallway.

I stuffed my bag in the locker, shut the door and promptly forgot to look at the number or remember the location. I got to the living room just in time to see all the kids file into the dining room.

"John, you can sit at table five," she pointed, "over there in the corner." I found a chair, which faced back into the room where I could see everything that was going on.

The matron said, "Be seated." Chairs screeched and groaned as they were filled and yanked to the table. As if by some silent signal all was quiet.

"Bow your heads for grace." Everyone put his head forward; I did the same. From across the room I could hear, "Bless us O Lord and these, Thy gifts, which we are about to receive through Thy bounty, through Christ, our Lord. Amen."

The silence was broken with "Pass the potatoes," "After

you on the gravy." "First dibs on seconds for the hot dogs." "I
get second dibs." "You want some potatoes, Kid?" I glanced
at the kid next to me as he shoved a large steaming bowl of
mashed potatoes under my nose. . . "Take some and pass 'em
on, will ya?"

I shoved in the spoon, flicked the potatoes on my plate
and before I was finished the bowl left my hand. "Pass 'em
on, will ya? Think you're the only guy at the table, huh?" I
passed the spoon to him, grabbed the hot dogs and was soon
initiated into the fastest food service in my life. Everything
was passed around once.

It took me some time to catch on to "dibs on seconds." I
soon learned whoever said "dibs" first got the first chance at
whatever was left over in that particular dish. If I wanted
seconds with no "dibs" I asked for the dish. Sometimes I got
what I saw and sometimes other guys helped themselves before
it got to me. I always got firsts, but seconds were never for
sure.

I tried answering all the questions the kids threw at me
but I floated in anxiety of what would happen next.

The matron dismissed each table. Everyone took out their
own dishes, glass and silverware. I got in line and headed
toward the kitchen. With 30 other kids in your hall the best I
got was, "Do like the other kids do."

Again, the friendly arm of the matron was on my shoulder.
"John, you can help with cleaning the tables tonight." She
patted me on the back as I entered the dining area.

"You can have table five, Kid," someone yelled. I thought
that was pretty good of them. It wasn't until I discovered table
five was furthest from the kitchen and by the time I got there

the other kids had loaded it with all the extra dishes. After endless trips back and forth I was yelled at.

"Hurry up, Kid, I gotta set the table; gonna take all night?" He stood there with two fists full of paper napkins and silverware. I hurried.

I watched the room change from full of kids to empty. All tables re-set as if nothing had taken place and ready for another meal. Things happened so fast I hardly had time to take part in them. It was my initiation into the hall assignment system where everyone is given a job, does it, gets it done and gets out.

It was quiet in the dining hall; it seemed to be what I needed. The matron came up to me, opened her arms and without hesitation I was absorbed in them. Tears swelled into my eyes and the warmth of her holding kept me together.

"Do you remember your locker number?" she asked. I shook my head in bewilderment.

"Come with me. I'll get you a towel and washcloth. Keep them in your locker. You only get one set a week so don't lose them."

As she walked down the hall, I followed and received a soft white towel and white washcloth. I thought this wouldn't be too hard to remember until I saw that everyone had the same size, color and shape. "Your locker is number 24. Now I'll show you your bed."

We went down the hall to a single door opening to what I thought would be a bedroom. It was a dormitory. My eyes glistened as I took in this huge room, double bunk, steel-spring beds on both sides. They seemed without end. She moved down the aisle to the far end and finally stopped at the second to the last bed.

"This is yours. You sleep on the bottom."

Had she said "top" I don't know what I would have done. The top bed was almost above my reach. How would I ever crawl into it if I had to?

"Bob is on top . . . He's from the city, just like you. You'll be just fine." She left me. I was deep in concern how I would remember everything; locker number 24, bottom bed, table number five what else would be new?

I was suddenly shocked by the blast of the steam whistle; it seemed to be right in the room with me. I walked to the hallway, just in time to be pushed aside by all the kids running to the locker room. Steel doors banged opened and shut. As if by robot action, they popped out naked, towel in one hand and washcloth in the other and headed down the hall in the opposite direction of the dormitory. They stood in line, flicking towels at one another, poking, laughing; as one wet head came out of the room, a dry one went in.

"Get your towel, kid. You gotta take a shower, ya' know?"

I undressed, piled my clothes in the locker, grabbed my towel and washcloth, tried covering myself and headed down the long hall. I was hoping some kids were left in line so I would know what to do. As I entered the room some kids were bent over a long sink that had three faucets on each side, they were brushing their teeth. I followed the line into another room, put my towel on a metal hook and got under a steaming shower.

"Here's some soap." A kid handed me a slippery bar of white soap.

"Thanks," I replied.

"Just got here today, huh?"

"Yeah."

"I've been here for almost a year. You'll get used to it. What's your name?"

He stared at me. "John," I blurted out.

"Mine's Bob. What locker ya' got?" he questioned.

"Number 24."

"Hey, that's right next to mine. I'm 25. How about that."

I slopped around trying to keep my balance, turned off the shower 'cause Bob did,' and went for my towel.

"Your tooth brush is number 24, too. Gotta brush your teeth after ya' shower."

Bob was frothing at the mouth. I grabbed the brush, put paste on it and scrubbed while I read the tube, "Dr. West Tooth Paste." After brushing and placing the brush back on the hook I wondered how they knew I needed one, or did it belong to another kid? With my towel wrapped around my middle I hurried to follow Bob down the hall to the locker room. I stuffed my towel in the locker, closed it, and followed his naked body into the dormitory. He headed in the same direction as my bunk.

"You down here, too?" he asked.

"Yeah." I pointed to the lower bunk.

"Hey, that's funny, I'm on top." He laughed, grabbed under his pillow and pulled out a long, white, cotton nightgown. In one twist he had it over his head and ran down the aisle out of sight.

I reached under the pillow and found the same kind of nightgown. It was light and moved easily as I walked. I never questioned a nightgown in all my years at Mooseheart. I learned to sleep in it, turn in it without twisting it or myself in knots and lived in one till I graduated at 18.

What surprised me was the sudden quiet in the hall. I was struck with the fear that everyone had gone and I was left alone. I ran down the hall, turned the corner and before I could stop, stumbled over the bodies that were lying on the floor.

"Gee whiz, kid; ya' dumb or something? Watch where you're going." "Shut up, you guys." "Oh, for crying out loud, just when the good part comes."

I lay where I landed and didn't dare move. From the corner of the room the radio was turned loud and I heard, "The Adventures of Jack Armstrong, The All American Boy, sponsored by Wheaties. Have you had your Wheaties today?"

Jack Armstrong thus became one of my heroes. He could do everything and secretly became a part of every boy who crowded around on the floor to hear his brave deeds. There was no question in anyone's mind that to eat Wheaties, as the advertising blared, would make him strong and unconquerable, bursting with physical prowess.

The quiet was particularly satisfying to me. It was the first time it was still since I entered the hall. I half-listened and let my eyes wander around taking in this group of white, ghost-like kids with whom I was to live for the rest of my formative life. I could see some faces; the rest were merely eyes that would meet mine. Others were in deep concentration on the story and lastly were those who were merely legs and bodies crossed and curled in positions hidden from me.

When the commercial returned they moved to life only to resettle when the story resumed. As the program ended someone yelled, "Turn to the Long Ranger, he's next." And with the sound of "Hi, Ho, Silver, Away" everyone yelled, "Hi, Ho, Silver, Away," then laughed, socked one another and settled down.

Wheaties were on the breakfast table the next day along with the Lone Ranger's picture on "Silvercup, the World's Finest Bread."

The intensity of these listening periods was felt throughout our lives. Our imagination was on the wavelength of constructing the West, of being with the Lone Ranger as he performed his good deeds. This unflinching, forever-justice individual did almost as much to develop our individual character as any human teacher. He became a part of our lives as much as did any person in the school.

We knew there were the good guys and the bad guys. We desired the innate attachment to feel justice accomplished, learned to hear the play of words in our imagination; it was like a string of beaded wisdom we could all count and arrive at the same moral conclusion.

We heard words which formed concepts and pictures in our minds as surely as if we had seen them on a movie screen. They became individual to each one of us. We were unified in another way that seemed to unknowingly bind us in a common purpose of living.

When the program was over and we were satisfied that the good guys won over the bad guys, we'd say, "Gee that was dirty nifty." Somehow our character was built by the words we heard over the radio.

"Okay boys, time for bible study. Get your books and let's settle down." The matron moved easily among us to her large rocking chair. The whistle blew and everyone became quiet and started to read. I looked around and not a word was spoken.

"John." I looked at the matron. She motioned for me to come to her.

"You're a Catholic. When you go to school this week be sure to ask the Father for your catechism. We have bible study every night except Friday and Saturday and you'll have to study your lessons. You just sit tonight."

She patted me on the shoulder. I leaned against her leg and she slowly rocked back and forth in her big chair. 1 was glad for the moment of feeling close to someone.

In fifteen minutes the whistle blew. It seemed to be in direct connection to every kid for they all instantly started in motion as if set by springs. The cook brought a large platter of cookies into the room; they disappeared before she could return with milk and glasses. It was a time for play before bed. I slowly ate my cookie, sipped my milk and watched 30 bodies tumble and toss in laughter and wrestle.

Darkness soon filled the sky outside. A long blast on the steam whistle indicated 9:30 P.M., which meant, all bodies in bed. The matron coaxed some and scolded others to move on, eventually all headed down the hallway. After being shoved down the aisle, I plopped on my bed, crawled under the sheet and pulled it up around my neck. Bob came running down the aisle, the matron's words following him,

"You get in that bed, Bob, or I'll come sailing down there after you."

He put one foot on my mattress, pushed hard and gripping his top bunk propelled him into the air and landed on his bunk. Everything was quiet. I could see the springs above me bend with Bob's weight. Suddenly his head popped over the side.

"You okay, huh?"

Through a glassy haze I murmured, "Yeah, okay."

I watched the leaves paint a moving picture on the wall as the street lamp silhouetted them. I slowly faded into rest, trying not to think of what would happen the next day.

Structure of Daily Life

The sun softly lit the dormitory. My eyes followed the long row of beds observing the bumps of bodies in curls, the upper-bunk mattress drooping into the springs. Bob turned and I watched the springs stretch and shrink and finally settle like a sagging bag. The cool early morning air was refreshing. The day before flashed through my head in a quick parade of confusing events. Before I could get too involved or cry over my bewilderment, I saw the matron coming down the aisle. She paused by my bed.

"Good morning, John." She sat on my bed, patted my arm. "I thought you could get up early before the rest of the kids and help make toast in the kitchen. Make your bed, wash up and get dressed." She left me.

The early silence gave me a chance to get myself together.

Bob poked his head over the side. "What ya' doing?"

"Gotta make toast."

"Don't burn it. I hate burnt toast."

The kitchen was warm, cozy and full of good smells. The cook was at the big, black stove, large pans were full of eggs and a griddle full of pancakes sent their steam down the hall to the dorm. Without looking up she pointed the frying spoon at the corner table and said, "Bread is over there. Don't burn the toast."

I opened the long loaf, the bread spilled out. I had never made toast before. I plopped six pieces on the iron grill rods, shoved it under the fire, and closed the door to the oven. There was no way I could see what was happening inside. As I opened the door to check a small black cloud of smoke caused me to cough. The toast was blackened. I flipped it over and soon matched the other side. This happened twice more.

The cook suddenly appeared and asked, "What's wrong?" She looked closely at me. "Oh, you're new. Leave the door open and when you see it get brown take it out." She grabbed a dish; "Here's the butter. Don't burn anymore." She returned to her stove.

I tried slice after slice; some brown, some black; I scraped what I could. She looked them over. "They're half-done and half burned. You're not supposed to burn them. Put them on the tray over there."

How not to burn toast was a lesson I learned later from another kid who was skilled at watching the heat coming from the stove. And thus it became apparent to me, day by day, that living in the hall was a process of how to survive on one's own.

The steam whistle shrieked through the hall and was soon followed by 30 pair of bare feet pattering down the hallway to the washroom.

Other kids started floating in and out of the kitchen. The milk was poured into large pitchers, one for each table. The eggs, pancakes, toast and meat followed the milk to the table.

After grace was said the food made the circle around the table. It wasn't as noisy as supper. I had a full plate of food and just as I reached for the toast some kid yelled, "Who made the burnt toast?" I held the plate suspended in front of me . . . all eyes at table five were glued on me. I noticed that I was holding a nicely toasted piece of bread. Very skillfully the toast was taken from my hand and as it made the round from hand to hand the burnt piece came the other way and was slipped between my fingers; the plate of breakfast food was snatched away from me.

As I bit into the dark toast I heard, "Learn to make good toast, kid." With plenty of milk to wash it down I realized I could hardly tell how burnt it really was.

Everyday started when the steam whistle blew at 6:30 a.m. Unbeknownst to me, my mind was slowly, but permanently getting conditioned to responding throughout each day according to the unrelenting punctuality of this whistle. When it blew, things happened or stopped happening. Right now I was to be out of bed, make my bed, put the nightgown under the pillow, get dressed, go to the toilet, wash my face, comb my hair, look at the assignment list and remember it.

The assignment sheet was a positive influence in my life. Through it, each child developed a good attitude toward work and felt the dignity of reward for a job well done. As others depended upon my job, I was to learn what I did and how I did it was important to the well being of my group. We held together or fell apart on our own efforts. The idea that it was work as such, or pure labor, did not occupy my mind. It was something I had to do, get at it, get it done and go on to something else.

I was scheduled to clean the dining room tables after breakfast, sweep the dining room floor after lunch and set table five after dinner for breakfast the next day. As I looked over the entire list I saw: scrub kitchen floors, wash dishes, rinse dishes, dry dishes, help cook, dust the living room, sweep locker room, collect towels, wash mirrors, scrub toilets, empty trash cans; the list covered every possible job that could be done in the hall to keep it in good order. I learned to do all the jobs, to excel at them or do them over, to contribute my effort to the group or get extra duty to make up for my lack of effort. Thus passed each day.

Getting acquainted with the other kids wasn't quite the problem it could have been. Being thrown into a working and eating schedule, together with the regulation of the hall routine, I soon found myself bumping into every other kid four or five times a day. The routines were so regular and repetitive that it soon seemed I had done these jobs for weeks and weeks. I soon forgot that life existed any other way.

It wasn't long until I was snapping my towel at another kid's rear end and the matron was yelling my name with great familiarity.

The assignments were part of everyone's life from Baby Village through 12th grade. But there was a sense of pride developed from this process that never openly expressed itself, but it was there, developing in each child each and every day. There was no better way of getting work done than by doing it yourself. We soon learned the same goes for pride; develop it by doing it yourself.

Over the years this routine became part of our very being and somehow became the ingredient that bound us together.

The hall in which I lived became something greater than its parts, with the end result that a matron, a cook and 30 boys were able to exist in harmony with destruction and conflict unknown quantities.

∽

REQUISITIONS

I was neatly dressed and had no shortage of clothes. I don't mean I could be careless; I had to be darn careful. When I outgrew or wore out any clothes, I would get a requisition from my matron and take it to the boy's store.

The man in charge would ask, "Well, what color would you like?," as he pointed to a small pile of shirts on the shelf. "Any of these will fit you. You can pick what you like." I looked at them. There were only six, in different colors, but all in the same design. Not much choice.

"I don't care," I responded," give me two." He grabbed two off the top, shoved them into a brown bag, signed my slip and handed them to me.

Mrs. Shuey met me with, "We'll have to be sure your laundry number is in your shirts. What is it, D-what?" "D-166," I blurted out. I watched as she took the special marking ink and scratched the black fluid inside the collar. It was there for good, through a hundred washes if necessary, until the threads started to pull apart and the shirt ended up in the ragbag in the basement. Many times I would be dusting or washing windows and sure enough, there would be D-166

41

staring me in the face. Some shirts I really liked; others were just good rags.

The shoe store was way in the back of the Boy's Store. My shoes were heavy, over my ankle, with very thick soles and seemed to last forever. About the only time I wore short shoes was for dress occasions, and then one had to be a big kid to get a pair of shoes like that.

My changes in life were very definitely related to the clothes I wore. As a young kid, I wore cut-off short pants during summer; as a teen-ager, knickers that buckled at the knee or just below. Color wasn't a determining factor; they were all khaki. Big kids wore long pants. I could tell when I reached certain ages of development when my shoes changed; I got long pants and started to shave. The young kids seemed to know that I was big.

~

Free to Wander and Wonder

THE LAKE

The lake was big, about a mile and a half around. It was my greatest delight to spend the entire morning there, go home for lunch, return and not leave until the steam whistle tooted me back to the hall for supper.

The lake wasn't an easy place to get around. Oh, it had a good road. I could even bicycle around it if I wanted to; cars made it in no time at all. But to walk around it seemed to take forever; there was just so much to see and do.

A lot of the doing sometimes was just sitting along the bank of the lake, watching the water ripple, getting my feet wet, lying back watching the clouds or just spending a few hours daydreaming. I'm sure a lot of who I am is the result of having had the time to go to the lake and enjoy just simply being there.

The trees were thick and colorful; the grass, long and shaggy. Lilac fragrance filled the air and when the birds sang, life became a pure joy. The feeling of this joy and the memory of it were to remain with me for the rest of my life.

As I walked down the hill by the priest's house, 1 would

come upon the water splashing over the dam. It was the only place from which I could see the entire lake from the dam to the other end where the creek started. There was a particular fascination in looking at the lake from the dam. I never got tired of watching the water move over the dam, the way it splashed on the rocks or just never seemed to come to an end; it was always changing but always the same. The dam was an endless occupation, easily deserving a good portion of the morning's time before I could do anything else.

I always climbed down the big wet rocks on both sides of the dam; it was a good place to catch fish because they found plenty of food from the water as it splashed over the rocks. The water was deep, but not so deep that I couldn't touch bottom.

It seemed to me there was always a watchman around the dump but hardly ever around the dam. The water was very deep at the top, just before it spilled over. Some of the other boys would walk along the top of the dam, like a tightrope walker. One false move and he would fall 30 feet into the rocks below or into the 30 feet of deep water on the other side. The challenge was there for the taking, many took it, I never did.

The trees by the dam sheltered a small green grapevine that produced lip-puckering grapes. I remember Mrs. Wolly scolding me in the classroom, "Take that gum out of your silly mouth." It wasn't gum at all. It was the long, twisty, grapevine endings from the lake. They had the sourest taste ever at first, but turned into the longest tasting, string-like fibers I ever chewed on, even better than celery.

At the point where the lake curled and slowed, were slimy

weeds that sheltered all sort of small snails. It was a haven for water spiders and all sorts of small water bugs lived there. The frogs lived closest to the shorelines.

The fresh-water spring by the old pussy willow marsh was always good for a drink of cold, fresh water. It was the only area around the lake that I really feared. It was swampy, with big dragonflies. The older kids told me that if I got too close to one it would sew up my lips. The dragonflies were everywhere.

The cattails around there grew so high it was hard to see the pine trees by the road. Many times I felt I was lost and would never get back to my hall. No one would ever find me if I should stumble and get sucked down by all the slimy weeds and stinking mud.

I loved the woods, the elm trees, how they changed so many colors during the fall . . . the maples and their winged-tipped seeds as they propelled themselves to the ground. The birch trees with their black and white bark. I used to peel it off and make small bark canoes. Oh, the leaves would turn so yellow, delicate and veined as the cold came, and they would fill the sky with fluttering gold. Yes, I was in love with the forest.

Maybe it was the trees and how they changed from so big when I got there and so small when I looked back. My perspectives of life changed in unison with the forest, as I grew older. It was always a part of my understanding.

I loved the violets and dandelions, the colors that dotted and patched the soft, willowy grass. I especially liked the lilacs and how we brought so many to the hospital when our matron got sick that the whole floor smelled like perfume.

There were too many sights and sounds of the forest to pass through it quickly. By throwing rocks, smelling flowers, having carp fights, making willow whistles and watching tad poles change from one stage of life to another, I took the first steps toward growing up and being more of what was me.

Once when we were shooting slingshots at birds a kid asked, "Suppose there wasn't a lake?" I recall the long silence and the lack of an answer. We just could not think of our lives without a lake. It was as much to us as we were to ourselves.

Walking in the woods during a rain was unique unto itself. Pearled water dropped from leaves. It started on the stem and changed color as it flowed over the veins, from deep red to rust and into lemon-yellow, eventually dropping into my mouth as I held the leaf, clean and clear, the colors disappearing as if by magic.

The lake would become pebbled as raindrops pierced the surface. Worms left the earth to cleanse themselves of their long, dirty diggings. Leaves twisted and turned, releasing themselves in the sound of color twirling to the earth.

The trees bobbed their boughs to one another, shaking their branches of any dust and dirt, happy in the exhilaration of the movement in contrast to the approaching stillness of a sunny day.

I never tired of being at the lake. It changed and with each change I changed. In the summer the juice of my growth flowed and expanded like the limbs of the trees. I became taller and reached closer to the sky as they did. During the autumn, I prepared for the long silence of winter, when inner rest and reflection would eventually flow out into new life with the spring.

It was never easy to get around the lake . . . it was much easier for the lake to get around me. It ran almost like a river in and out of my life in an unceasing ebb and flow, never to leave me.

∾

THE DUMP

The dump was the one place that was the favorite at which to meet and do stuff. It was a paradise of everything from junk cars, old lamps, broken bed springs, magazines we weren't suppose to see because they were too trashy, rope, bailing wire, shoes . . . you name it, it was there. You could hit the dump either on your way out to the lake or on your return. It was handy either way.

There is something absolutely delightful and soul fulfilling about a dump. I don't know what it is, but it's a terrific place.

It was a place where shacks were built during the hot summer to keep cool and to keep warm in the freezing cold. There's something particularly challenging about constructing a shack without nails, just using lousy lumber, rusty wire, old sheet metal and boxes. The watchman always cautioned us, "One of these days that shack is going to fall on your head and someone's going to get hurt." Never did. We never built one to ever fall down. One even stayed up for so long we called it, "The Cave." We roasted enough parched corn in there to feed every kid at the orphanage for a full year.

Parching corn takes no cooking skill. Just take an old tin can (not rusty), wrap a wire around it, drop kernels of dried corn in the bottom and hold it over a fire. When it begins to smell burned, it's done. There's nothing like it. On a cold day I would fill my pockets and chew on it all day long.

If a fight started in the hall or classroom all ears would perk up and we'd finally hear, "Oh, yeah! Meet me at the dump and say that."

Now there's nothing so discouraging to a good fight as having to walk half a mile to have it. Then, again, it was a good excuse to go to the dump.

Of course, girls couldn't go to the dump; it was on the boys' campus. We had the lake, dump, nursery, farm, arboretum and the football field; everything was on the boys' campus except baby village, and who wanted that.

I was amazed that everything I ever wanted to do was by the dump. A small stream ran right through it. We used it for drinking all the time. It wasn't until the school started taking out the nursery that we discovered it was the run-off water they used to water all the plants and bushes. It wasn't until then we started to question whether or not it was fit to drink. A kid said the science teacher told him the water should be boiled to kill the germs and allowed to cool. Then it was okay to drink. We started taking large, empty gallon tomato juice cans to fill full of water and then boil. This proved too much bother and we ended up scooping the water to drink with our hands the way we always did.

Strangely enough, the dump served as a tempering influence upon my youth as well as a place to smoke newspaper and corn silk, parch corn and build shacks. Certain areas somehow got to be known as Crows Place, Hill Top, and Gully Hollow. It was just understood that these territories and all the junk in each belonged to a certain gang. Of course, lots of stealing went on when the other gang wasn't around. This was cause for some foul language, tin cans thrown at one another, some full of rocks. Other times, splintered boards crashed on the shacks, threats were made that held the fear of death if we ever trespassed on one another's property again.

I did a lot of growing up at the dump. Part of my education was in the junk I found, how I used it or misused it. And, part of the literature I read advanced my perspectives far beyond my years.

One of the advantages of having a nursery of young trees and a lake surrounded with older trees is the tremendous selection of crotches for slingshots. Although they were not allowed, slingshots were the pride and joy of every rock-loving boy. We had slingshot contests to see who could shoot a rock the farthest. There must be forty thousand stones in the lake, all shot from slingshots.

Slings were worth ten hours on Special if we got caught; they were weapons, said our advisors. We didn't think so until we outlawed slings ourselves during rabbit shagging season. Too many boys got hit and the rabbits got away. Some of the stones were like bullets.

The biggest crotch I can remember we ever tried to make found its beginnings in the dump. We split a car inner tube into two three-inch strips, each about three feet long. The crotch was from a dead tree limb, so big we had to dig a hole to support the base. We tied the rubber tube to each upright limb and wired it tight with some bailing wire. The pocket was made from an old leather purse we found. Two guys held the crotch while two others put a tin can in the pocket. The rubber was pulled back about four feet and the can went sailing off into the horse pasture. We were elated.

We tried a heavy stone, small in size; it zoomed into the stream. After much yelling and picking up of odd-size objects, we decided to try a house brick. It fit neatly into the pocket of the sling. The two guys on the crotch gripped it so it wouldn't turn, even had their feet propped against it for good measure. The sling was pulled back and someone yelled, "Further, it needs more power." The further the rubber was pulled the more tense and quiet we became. "Here it goes." One of the guys holding the crotch turned to see what was happening. It moved off angle, the rubber slipped and the brick whistled by his head hitting his thumb. He had a smashed thumb and wore a steel splint around it for almost six weeks. We didn't try giant slingshots anymore.

After a hard days work of plowing and doing the farm chores, the farmers used to leave the big plug horses in the big field between the nursery and the cemetery. The horses were left to graze and rest. This wasn't exactly a good decision for it gave us another diversion and provided endless fun that made going to the dump even more enticing.

Most of us had never been near a horse, let alone ride one. The animals were very gentle, slow and friendly. A hand full of corn from our parched corn supply was enough to coax them to the fence. As a horse slobbered all over our hands to get the corn, a boy would jump off the fence post onto its back. This was worth a good leisurely stroll around the field.

After a few weeks of this, we got more courage. Observing how the farmers used rope to steer them, we made head gear ourselves. Of course, the smarter we got the more discontented the plugs became. We now rode them full speed, whacking their rear-ends with a rope and playing cowboys and Indians. Eventually the hospital received a few broken arms that were hard to explain. The farmers caught us, after wondering why after all the rest the horses were getting they were still so tired. We all got 15 hours on Special, spending all our free time at labor until the total 15 hours were worked off.

RABBIT-SHAGGING

Rabbit-shagging season started just about the time leaves began to drop from the trees. Almost every kid at the school had a lump on his leg at one time or another from shagging rabbits.

I had all sorts of rabbit clubs. When I was young the club was a single piece of 2 x 4, about a foot long. I rubbed the handle against a brick until it was round and smooth. Once, I heated a long rod of steel in the dump fire and burned a hole in the bottom of the wood. After spending hours looking for old lead tire weights, I melted them and filled the hole. This gave weight to the club so that when it was thrown it really stayed on course. Other boys would pound nails into the club and let the heads stick out. Getting hit in the leg with it meant a sure trip to the hospital. It wasn't the bandage that was so bad; it was trying to answer the nurse's questions about how in the world you ever got that way.

During the summer the rabbits built their runs and nests under the bushes. Rabbits wore brown coats during summer and changed to a light honey color in winter. It was hard to find them anytime.

We had what we considered a foolproof scientific way of getting rabbits. A group of boys would go up to the shack at the top of the hill, spread out and come yelling like mad, hitting the bushes along the way, scaring the rabbits. This way the rabbits would leave their nesting places and run toward the other end. The rest of us would be standing there, clubs in hand, waiting for the first rabbit to come. As soon as we'd see one, someone would surely yell, "Rabbit" and all the clubs would start flying in that direction. You'd think fifty clubs was plenty for one little rabbit. Sometimes it was and other times some kid would get mutilated and start limping in the direction of the hospital.

If we didn't get the rabbit running downhill to the dump we reversed the procedure, started yelling and beating the bushes hoping to scare up another one.

After we shagged rabbits for a couple of years we got pretty good at it. We soon learned to spread out on all four sides of the nursery and practice throwing the clubs before rabbit-shagging season started, along with perfecting our methods of constructing clubs.

The rabbits were skinned right there in the field. Not many boys had knives because they were not allowed, but whomever had one got the job of skinning. The rabbit was always pissed first. This meant running your finger down hard from the belly to the rear end. This eliminated all the urine so it wouldn't get on the meat once it was opened. The knife was then pushed right under the ribs and on down through the hind legs. All the guts would spill out. Someone said to be sure to check the kidneys for yellow spots. This would mean the rabbit was sick and shouldn't be eaten. We always checked but never did find any yellow spots.

The next step was to cut the fur around the back legs and grab hold of the skin, while another boy held the legs. He could rip the skin right off the rabbit up to his head. The last thing was to cut off the head and the rabbit was ready for cooking. We kept the skins, scraped the inside and let them dry for a couple of days in the sun. There's really nothing so soft as a rabbit skin; I could rub my hand over it for hours.

Since we were next to the dump, the rabbit usually cooked in a short time. There was always a fire; trash burned every day. The rabbit was cut up into pieces and stuck on ends of bailing wire and hung over the fire. The place was all smoky and boys were forever coughing, running out of the shack to get a breath of air. That didn't stop us; there was nothing as tasty as fresh, roasted rabbit.

After we sat there and got thawed out, rested and ate the rabbit, we were ready to go again. Sometimes we had to wait while a few boys rolled dried corn silk in newspaper and had a smoke.

If the day was good we'd get ten rabbits, roast and eat them, find some good junk and head for the halls when the whistle blew for supper.

THE BROWN CANDY BAG

The most popular place around on Saturday was the Boys' Store. After our hall duties were completed we got our weekly allowance of five cents. Nothing, and I mean nothing, had priority once that nickel was in my hand. I was aimed at the Boys' Store and didn't stop till I pushed open the door. There on the glass counter were brown bags of mixed candy, the tops twisted shut and all lined up so neat and nifty.

I plunked my nickel on the glass, waited for it to be picked up and listened very carefully for those magic words, "Okay." My hand circled the twisted top and the candy was mine.

I went to the side of the building, opened the bag to discover what candies were inside. My fingers caressed the soft chocolates, pushing aside the nickel-wafers and the Power House bars. The penny candy served to satisfy my craving for sweetness.

It seemed only natural that every kid would bend over his candy bag, stuff his mouth with something he liked best before taking time to look around for the other kids. Since all the bags had a variety of candy in them it was time to trade off the stuff you didn't like so well for other good stuff.

This was the biggest Jewing session you ever saw. Kids were trading five nickel-wafers for special jellies, Snicker Bars for Power Houses, Three Musketeers for assortments of hard candy. There's no doubt in my mind that part of growing up is trading stuff for other good stuff! It just didn't seem to matter, there was always somebody who liked the junk you hated and you liked the junk he hated.

What always surprised me was how much candy was still around during the middle of the week. I rationed my nickel-wafers to my tongue, one in the morning, one at noon, and one at night. Many are the times I sucked on hankies or shirts for a chocolate bar that melted in my drawer when I forgot about it.

$\backsim$

TAD POLES, CATTAILS AND APPLES

The spring of the year caused a shortage of jars, both in the halls and at the dump. Along the side of the road by the pulley crossing was a cattail pond. Nowhere in the world were there more tadpoles than here. They were swimming around by the hundreds. I had a jar full of them by my bed, one in my locker. I spent hours watching this little bigheaded animal wiggle itself up and down the glass. Day by day it began to show bumps on its side, the tail got smaller. Eventually little legs tickled the water and a four legged, half-tailed animal replaced the small black blobs. About this time they needed air and it seemed only appropriate to bring them to school and put them in a girl's desk, between the pages of a book or just hand them to a girl and have her grab it before she knew what was going on.

The matron also had locker cleaning day when the smell in the basement became too foul. We kept bottles in secret places by the basement lockers only to be discovered when the smell became so bad it was no trouble at all to find them.

The cattails adorned the art room and served as still life art models. They stood straight and tall in jars, contrasting well with daisies and ferns and pleased the art teacher to no end. As a gift to the matrons, they were placed in tall jars and appeared on corner tables, atop pianos and in the kitchen nooks.

As if by some magical signal the complete dryness of a cattail and the need for a boy to swing something occur at the same moment. The halls thus became barren of this tall popsicle-like stick as we used them to hit each other on the head, rear ends and body. There must have been ten million cattail seeds floating in the sky; they reflected like spun glass. The entire atmosphere seemed fractured; the seeds rode the wind as if a phantom hand guided them.

In the classroom it was a different story. The teacher, believing the punishment should fit the crime, had us carefully pick up one seed at a time, place it in the trash can then get another and another until the room was clean. On those days we missed both recess and lunch.

Stealing apples somehow enhances their taste. I just couldn't resist tucking my pant legs into my socks and loading the legs with apples until my belt would no longer stay in place. With such an abundance of fruit I kept eating and eating until I felt like bursting. There is something about early, green apples, when added to water, have a way of swelling up inside the stomach. I felt lousy, like throwing-up. Wouldn't you know it, Ole Man Peters, the watchman, came driving up the road?

When he asked me to get in the front seat next to him my darn pant leg slipped out of my sock and that saved me from answering his next question.

After he helped me up the stairs to the hospital and the nurse pumped out my stomach, I awoke in bed. On the top of the iron bedrod was a piece of paper stuck there with some adhesive tape. It was upside-down, but I could still read the message: 'Report to Dean of Boys, Trespassing-Private Property-Apple Orchard.' I groaned and rolled over thinking I should fake being sick a little longer.

SPECIAL

I don't know of anyone who was not on Special at one time or another. "Special" meant giving up free time after school, all day Saturday and Sunday and being assigned to do any work that needed to be done until one's hours were served.

Anticipating going to the Dean's Office was a mixture of odd emotions. I knew it meant punishment. For those who never had to suffer this self-propulsion and receiving their ill-earned reward were denied an element of growth.

"Come in, come in." The Dean always sounded so glad to see me, just as though nothing had happened.

"I understand you were caught stealing apples in the Apple Orchard on private property".

"Yeah, the watchman caught me."

"I understand you made a quick trip to the hospital. You okay now?"

"Yes. Everything is fine now."

My eyes wandered from his and settled on the plaque on his wall. It was a beautiful gold frame with special printing. I read, 'Be The Best You Can Be.'

"Are you pretty good at shining brass, cutting lawns?"

"Pretty good," I replied.

"That's fine. I think Mr. Burns would appreciate some help around the sidewalks and in the auditorium."

I reached out, took the paper, thanked him and followed the long hall that lead in the direction of the auditorium. I read the paper, 'On Private Property.' In the right hand corner was boldly written, '15 hours.' My arms started to ache.

Mr. Burns always sat in the first seat behind the brass rail closest to the stage in the auditorium. I entered, gave my name, he checked it. We sat every other seat so we couldn't talk to one another. Sometimes we'd sit out all the time in silence. If we talked, "Peanut," as he was called, would clench his fist and raise the center-finger knuckle above the rest as a warning he would rap us on the head if we didn't shut up. I got it plenty of times. One knuckle rub and crack on the head was enough for a long, long time.

The jobs he had us do weren't the most exciting either. I must have scrubbed the boys' toilets 200 times. Carrying the mail was kinda nifty because we went into the halls; if I got the girls' campus that was a real treat. The boy's campus was lousy since it was so spread out.

I got Special for a hundred reasons: being on the girls' campus, a good share for being on the girls' side of the road; sling shots cost me about 50 hours; off campus, 20 hours; fighting, 10; on Private Property, 20; riding plug horses, 15; and another miscellaneous 100 hours for odd things I can't remember. It's a wonder I had time to get into trouble. It didn't seem to bother me too much because all of us had it figured to the minute when we would be free once again and made plots accordingly.

The real offenders, the bad guys, were sent to Fez Hall. Fez was half-a-mile up the road in the farm area away from the campus. Kids sent there lived there, didn't go to school or see anybody except the other guys who were in with them. Fez was no fun. They got up early, had breakfast and out to the fields they went; picking weeds, raking, doing farm chores morning to night. Evenings were spent doing schoolwork so the whole day was a real bummer.

Going to Fez meant at least one solid week; some guys got one month. The real long-term guys got the reputation and everyone knew; "Watch out, he was at Fez Hall. You monkey around with him and you've had it."

School

Going to school for the first time was as apprehensive for me as moving into the hall. My first day in school was my first day seeing girls and being with them. I was hardly aware that there were girls in the orphanage; at least, these thoughts were the furthest from my mind. Going to school was something I just did. I attended. It was part of the daily schedule and I never questioned or rebelled against it. I went.

Stuttering was a big problem with me. I don't know when it started or when it began getting to me, but it did. We always had to read out loud in class and sometimes that meant standing up in front of the class to read. One day I was called upon to do this.

"John, you read today. Start chapter five for us."

I was dressed in shorts, shirt and sloppy socks. My shoes clunked on the wooden floor of the temporary portable building and I faced the class.

"Cha-Cha-Chapt-T-Ter, Fa-Fa-Fa," I stuttered on until "Five" burst from my mouth like a bubble. I was excited and felt very closed in; there wasn't room for me to move around inside myself. The first sentence started.

"Th-Th-The . . . Ha-Ha-Ha-Ha-Horse, Cra-Cra-Cra," I stammered on, grabbing quick breaths hoping to push this out of me and get it over quick.

"Cro-CrCrossed Th-The-The-Th-," I stuttered and stammered forcing each letter out of my throat, over my tongue and finally chopped it beyond my teeth. My eyes continued to stare at the page and somehow the words continued to come from deep within me.

"John, do you want to read later?" questioned the teacher.

"Na-Na-No-No," I snapped back. "Th-Th-Th-Th- Ho-Ho-Ho-Horse . . . Cr-Cr-CrosCrossed . . . Th-Th-Th-," I hesitated and attacked the, "Pa-Pa-Pa-Pa-Past-T-Tu-Tur-Ture." Tears filled my eyes, my stomach was full and I felt like I was going to throw up. My legs were wet with sweat and itched. The teacher apparently came up toward me but I didn't see her. I stuttered on "Th-Th-Th."

Suddenly, I felt a hand on my shoulder. I turned quickly, kicked violently at her legs, threw my book at the wall, sobbed and ran down the aisle, stabbed open the door and flew out into the cool morning air.

At the Bug House, I met Mr. Fatheringham. He took me upstairs, told me to lie down on a small cot in the corner. He began talking to me, slowly, very deliberately. We met once a week and each time he tried to get me to relax.

"Let your body go limp; first your feet, then come up to your ankles." It seemed to me I was being put to sleep. Just when I was about ready to fall off he started asking me questions. I don't remember any of the questions but my time on the couch became less and less and I soon found myself sitting at a table. I never did find out why he had me do such things as trace squares and circles, all sorts of things while looking into a mirror. We also spent a lot of time doing lip and tongue exercises along with lots of deep breathing. He asked me to use my lips and tongue more, saying, "Speak distinctly and with a slower speed."

I was fine in his office. When I was in school I just never volunteered for any reading in front of class. I never gave very many answers either. If I did, I made sure the words were not beginning with any T's, D's, or P's. If they ever came up I tried to stutter through them or change the words to other ones. This probably increased my vocabulary for I was forever hunting for new words that didn't have the hard initial letter for me to pronounce. Eventually the entire problem seemed to lessen. As with all kids, I was so involved in other parts of my life that I paid very little attention to stuttering. I was active in every school organization and very busy playing soccer. Even though the stuttering seemed to disappear, the same tension would always return under the pressure of public performances. In these times I would hesitate and do a fast substitution for difficult words so that stuttering would be less noticeable. The fact I was eventually cured of such a hand-icap changed my entire outlook on school. I slowly began participating in classes and felt "normal" like the rest of the kids.

As I grew older and entered high school I began to take enormous pleasure in my classes. There were all sorts of reasons. Literature, the words and how I reflected their meaning within myself. Math, the fascination of numbers and how the mystery of their usage became confusing in my head.

I flunked Math on paper, but, appreciated the beauty of what the numbers could do on paper and then became a reality in the form of a machine, an airplane or determine a perfect circle on a lathe.

Chemistry somehow always remained in the test tube, I couldn't see molecules or visualize the obvious that my instructor taught. Nevertheless, Science became one of my favorite subjects.

Each grade level pulled me through the eye of development with its own particular thread of fascination. My efforts were sincere. I did my homework and tried to fulfill the class demands. I once put my blanket over the window after lights-out and purposefully sat down at the table to do my Physics lesson. The struggle to resolve the principles and math brought me to the realization of the amount of absorption it took me to apply myself to the problem. In this act, I was finding another potential within myself, like a lost piece of puzzle being found or the "who I am" beginning to gain new perspective.

Because I was older this had a sharper edge to it. What seemed odd was how studying Physics could bring about this inner feeling. Despite the difficulty of such subjects, I learned to appreciate their application through inventions, in new ways of doing things. I have a tendency to attribute beauty or appreciation to these mysterious applications and turn them into an inner feeling.

The reading of Silas Marner stayed with me for a very long time. As each kid read a portion of the book I absorbed how he felt about the story. The teacher found it worthwhile to have us read aloud day after day until I could picture Silas just exactly the way he was drawn in the book illustrations. Strange, but the fine-lined drawing seemed so real that they began to speak to me in the same words and descriptions as the printed page.

How such fine lines could make up a picture fascinated me. I followed them and studied how they ended up in the forms of a coat, shoe or fingers. I could not stay away from these pictures. I liked what they did to me. It was unlike anything color said or did to me.

There must be a special day or moment set aside when a boy meets a teacher who is his first love. My English teacher held that magic moment for me.

She smiled easily, greeted me at the door with, "Good Morning." The soft melodious quality of her voice, her bright teeth and soft red lips vibrated a something within me unlike any other emotion I had ever known. The usual demands of diagramming sentences, learning grammar, punctuation, became secondary to my purpose of being in her class. No lesson reached me so deeply as when she read to us. Her expression, the use of her hands, how she would casually close her fingers and suddenly fling them in the air expressing the story tossed me into the emotional and physical awareness that I could live this, the words, as vividly as though I were the character in the story.

I attended summer school, because she said, "Your grammar is so poor." I achieved poorly, but my need to be saturated in words and how they became part of my very being flourished.

Unknown to me, was the basic love I was developing and what she represented in being a woman. She was entirely unmale, courteous, kind, smelled good. She impressed me as 'her,' more spirit than as a body. Her aura and image were most overpowering. It was my first experience with this unique combination.

My life was changed. I felt good that she was part of me. It was to influence my relationship later with girls. I remember her as my first crush. I also treasure how reading and words were now magic and my thinking and seeing were more vivid.

$$\curlywedge$$

TEACHERS

There comes into each person's life one teacher or several who shape character and remain with you in their very individual ways for the rest of your life.

Mr. Deny was such a man. In his surroundings of the ornamental concrete plant, I learned to love statues, pictures and molds that were filled with plaster or marble, and when uncovered, one beauty after another appeared; benches, flower pots, religious busts, Corinthian columns. What would have been merely plaster on a wall became beauty in my soul because of him.

Deep within me was the desire to create, to take a lump of clay and shape it into form as if giving it life. Under his guidance I somehow ended up molding and shaping my own life, adopting the profound qualities of that unique teacher.

He was always dressed in a white, plaster-stiff pair of

coveralls; his pipe stank, his temper kind and gentle, then flaring as he threw a hammer at some kid because he was so damned obstinate about following directions that he had ruined a good mold pouring.

After years of seeing Mr. Deny in this role, I was dumbfounded when I saw him on the stage, dressed in a black suit and tie with words coming from his mouth that bespoke of appreciation and accomplishment of his students. He was above all a gentleman. I at last saw him as a person for the first time.

When I returned to the shop the next day and he asked me to fill his pipe, I packed it full of pure tobacco; leaving out the usual strands of string, small pieces of rubber bands and upholstery hair I often packed in. "This is really a good smoke, John. The best I've ever had from you."

He smiled at me, put his arm around my shoulder and walked me to the other end of the shop, all the time yelling at the other kids to "Get to work," "Pick up the clamp," "Get away from the saw," "Don't get any glue on the table." I had already worked like a horse all morning, but for Mr. Deny, I would have done anything he asked, anytime. He was part of me.

Mr. Deny, as with many other male teachers in school, served as an adopted father to me. Enough credit is never given to the role, often because the evidence is under the guise of the title of "teacher" or "coach." It was this person-to-person contact that was the difference.

The roles of the women in my life were as important as those of the men for I did not live with my mother at Mooseheart. These female teachers became mothers. As is true with any normal child, these women became, for me, the ideal as far as romance was concerned.

They were all fine people. They represented the outside world, people I saw only during school time, a brief period, but long enough to get deeply involved.

I remember reading; "I never knew I was poor until someone asked what it was like to be poor." In searching for the meanings in my life I discovered the riches I had didn't depend on money or things. I was rich from using and investing my creative talents with the support of my teachers. Making do with what I had was always part of my life. It was a preparation for the living of life that could have been denied me by over doting parents, or denied me had I been spoiled by other self-indulgent means. I never truly felt denied anything; I was too involved with living.

Every kid at Mooseheart was given from 9 to 18 weeks of introduction to the vocational training courses. They included electricity, sign painting, sheet metal, machine shop, printing, ornamental concrete, woodworking, arts and crafts, sewing, cooking, typing, shorthand, beauty parlor and others. By the time I was a junior in high school I was expected to pick one vocation of my choice and pursue this in detail so I would be able to go out into the world and get a paying job to support myself. It wasn't until I looked in the graduation program that I noticed all graduates' names were listed, according to the major area, pursued by each.

The environment of each course was a teacher in itself. The cement plant, print shop and cooking, each had a special aura. I became a sponge for the sights and smells and feelings of the places.

By means of the vocational system our work was displayed and used everywhere on campus. Light posts, benches, bird baths and marbleized planting boxes were all from the cement plant. Our paper from the print shop, signs from the sign-painting department, much of the food from the canning department. Courses were not exclusively for boys or girls although it was common that boys took 'men subjects' and girls stuck to the home courses.

Learning is not without some valuable lessons unforeseen and unplanned. One incident permanently fixed in my memory is about an electric popcorn popper that didn't work properly. Bob and I were checking the switch, contact points, the plug and long wire. Some small soldering was done. We were sure it was ready and Bob said, "Plug it in." He had the open wire basket in both his hands. I pushed in the plug and suddenly heard a loud gasp. Bob seemed to jump into the air, his hands extended forward as if offering popcorn to me, his eyes bugged, tongue hanging out, and his face completely white. It took me some time to gather my wits before I pulled the plug from the socket. The huge intake of air sucked into Bob caused quite a gathering of classmates, plus the instructor.

"Anything wrong here?" he questioned. Bob still had the wire basket burned to his fingers, extended, as if asking him to check if. He looked at it, checked the plug. "It works, huh?"

Bob choked out a, "Yeah, it works fine." Two of his fingers and one thumb had deep red lines along their length, like hot dogs kept on the fire too long. As we left the room Bob pointed to a sign on the wall, 'Read it, dummy.'

The sign said, 'Check before you plug in.' I always remember that sign now when I work with electricity.

The experiences were memorable. I came in contact with teachers of differing viewpoints who were practical and attempted to awaken the sense of money value in all us kids who had never paid for anything we had eaten, worn or enjoyed.

∿

SPORTS "ITS THE SPIRIT THAT COUNTS"

I sat in my seat, a white jersey shirt with Rambler stitched across the chest, a large #21 on my back. Soccer was my major sport. I was calm, but excited inwardly, this was my first trip away from Mooseheart.

I wasn't prepared for the large visitor's room, the awesome feeling it belonged to another team. A gutty sensation hit me that a battle was about to take place and I was in the middle. The coach started his usual patter of "watch number 3, cover him at all times, the goalie is fast but slow on the angle shots, and blah-blah blah." My head was spinning.

Once on the field I was now enclosed on three sides by bleachers, the stands full of cheering people, rooting for the other team. I froze; my mind was blank. Where were the trees and open field I was used to? The whistle blew and almost without knowing I was racing toward the ball, hit it with my head and heard someone yell, "That's the way, Crow, that's using your head."

My head was clear and what was fright passed away; there was just too much to do and think about. I ran across the field chasing the ball as though it were a personal responsibility that I be near it at all times. My subconscious mind kept dictating to my body the admonition of the coach, "Keep the ball low, pass to your closest teammate, don't try to be a hero, kick it, anticipate what the other guy will do, get the lead out, get moving." And so I shot from one end of the field to the other in an endless back and forth.

Our first goal gave us a positive feeling about the game. We were the underdogs. The other team spoke two languages. This, coupled with the fact they were all bigger than us, automatically threw us into a disadvantage. As the game progressed we got more and more injuries; the other team more and more fouls. With each injury we scored another goal. Somewhere within us was an inner drive, a faith that erupted into more energy and determination than ever before. The coach was yelling his head off but never with strategy . . . it seemed as if he had us tied to his mouth with a string and was able to shout something that reached us as individuals and we reacted to this personal tug. No matter what we did we just could not lose. Our feet and heads always pointed in the direction of the goal and the ball shot like a bullet into the net.

The score was 18 to 17, their favor. We made a score and it was even. I heard the captain of our team yell, "Hey, Crow." I looked up and the ball was flying through the air, I stopped it with a foot, started to dribble and head for the goalie. I shifted the ball from foot to foot, evading the goalie and lifted my foot for one last forceful drive at the net. The world went black. I heard a gun shot.

The lockers all came into perspective, my coach was leaning over me. "How do you feel?" he asked.

I sat up, feeling his arm around my shoulders, the other

guys quiet and standing around in a circle. I muttered, "Okay, I guess." Then the roar of my teammates echoed in my head. It wasn't until later that I learned I had kicked the final winning goal in the last two seconds of the game. The goalie had swung his arm across my nose and I was knocked out just as the gun signaled the end of the game.

It was good to get home. The next day all the guys razzed me about my black eye; the girls looked at me in a different way than before. My girlfriend squeezed my arm and stayed close to me even when other couples came by.

The coach asked how my eye was, gently touched it, put his arm around my shoulder and said, "You played a great game. That last shot was unbelievable."

The coaches seemed to change with the seasons but the story was always the same . . . how to play the game, the attitude, the drive, encouragement, and determinism. It stimulated all of us, just like new sap entering the trees at the first sign of spring. Somehow, all his yelling made sense. I thought he was great.

...And These Thy Gifts

THE TRUCK FARM

I never sat at the table and left hungry, there was always plenty of food; all the milk I cared to drink. When I was in 7th grade I began to share in the effort and labor it took to put this food on the table. I had been in the farm before, but this was when I climbed out the dorm window at night to steal watermelons from the patch near the hall.

My first assignment was on the farm truck that delivered fresh vegetables to the halls. As I copied a list for the garden report I was aware, for the first time, just what all the food delivery was about. My list read:

TOTAL of all vegetables sent from the garden in one year to halls or cannery.

Asparagus	6,237 bunches
Green Beans	6,674 lbs.
Beets	11,015 lbs.
Carrots	3,658 lbs.
Cabbage	23,027 lbs.
Cucumbers	7,367 lbs.

Sweet Corn	46,205 ears
Green Onion	2,894 bunches
Dry Onions	2,894 lbs.
Parsley	26 lbs.
Peas	185 lbs.
Potatoes	1,994 bushels
Tomatoes	46,598 lbs.
Turnips	586 1bs.
Chard	799 lbs.
Rhubarb	7,099 lbs.
Radishes	1,231 bunches
Lettuce	1,164 lbs.
Kohlrobi	531 lbs.
Squash	7,321 lbs.
Eggplant	65 lbs.
Celery	269 lbs.
Chi-clery	81 lbs.
Pumpkins	2,340 lbs.
Grapes	1,750 lbs.
Peppers	1,799 lbs.
Mongol beets for livestock feed	110 tons

The truck farm was a large 330 acres bounded by West Legion Hall, Fez Hall and the dump. Everything we ate came from the farm. What was not needed ended up at the cannery in the Vocational Building. Of course, there were farm hands, trucks and machinery to do all the hard work, but nothing did it better than us kids who had six weeks of idle time on our hands during summer vacation. You name it; we had our two hands in all of it.

As I entered the gate to the farm I noticed the varied colored plants, the long green beans, the wide leaves of the celery and the red rhubarb stems that made such good rhubarb sauce. I had a definite feeling about standing in front of my assigned row of tomatoes, and it wasn't good.

The foreman yelled, "Okay, when you get to the other end you're done. Be sure you pick every stinking weed or you'll get another row." I looked down the row and all I could see was an ocean of green leaves and red dots 'til they disappeared into one mass.

Some guy yelled, "Hey, that's Fez Hall way out there." That did it; Fez was a half-mile away. The thought of the job caused antagonism within me, and all sorts of resentment flowed.

Nothing more was said, I bent over and pulled the first weed, then another. After a long period of time, I stood erect, pushed my hands against a very aching back. I could see I had come a long way, the weeds showed definite patterns in the isle. This changed me somehow. I seemed to be less bothered by the labor.

My eyes concentrated on the tomatoes as my hands automatically reached for weeds and did their work. Some tomatoes are rich-red, some very dark; others light green, some small, hard and just beginning to develop. I began to feel them, learn of their life by touch. The very dark ones were soft and my fingers too easily pierced the skin; the juice oozed over my dirty hand. Obvious to me by now was the very distinct smell the stems gave when broken.

As I looked around the farm at the thousands of growing plants and the number of seeds in my hand right then, I was awed by the realization. The awareness of seeds and growing things suddenly came together and gave meaning to me as never before.

The sun was very hot, salty sweat curved over my cheeks and into my mouth. I sat in the dirt, absentmindedly reached for a tomato and pierced the skin with my teeth and sucked the juice. How delicious was this taste; how satisfying. I sucked it dry, my tongue mixing the salty taste of perspiration with the juice. I spent a great deal of time peeling the skin, observing seeds, veins and stem. I stared at the plant itself, noticing now the tomatoes hung in such a created order. How neat. How could this be done? When I threw the pulp on the ground and watched the pattern it made, I could hardly believe all this came from one seed and could grow more seed for more plants. My wonderment increased.

For the first time, I looked at my hands, how dirty they were; two broken fingernails, but more than anything else, how my fingers gripped weeds, closed around them, tugged and slapped the dirt away from the root. I did this slowly, many times. What a powerful machine the hand is. I was puzzled as to how many times my hands closed and opened just picking weeds.

The breeze chilled me from such a long rest. I started to weed again, looking through my legs; the row was straight as an arrow, the starting shack looked miles away. Peering ahead, the end was so close, or seemed to be. Whatever the cause I worked with a renewed strength, a desire to complete the job, to get every weed no matter how small. I was even more careful not to hit any stems or break them.

I threw the last weed into the air and watched it turn

lopsided circles and finally plop to the earth. Somehow I had no bitterness or antagonism, no tiredness; only a sense of exhilaration, of wonderment and even a sense of pride. I did it. Why did that mean so much to me? Three weeks later I had the same row, only this time I was picking red tomatoes and dropping them into a large basket, loading them on the truck and watching it head for the cannery. In a few months I would be eating them.

CANNERY

As soon as the large cannery doors opened I got my first whiff of steam, mixed with seasonings and all sorts of vegetable odors.

"OK. you guys, let's get to work. Boys, unload the corn from the truck, girls at the table. Jim, you work with me at the boilers. John, you work the cooling tanks. Ray, you do the lids for a while." The supervisor quickly organized us into areas and we routinely headed in the proper direction.

It wasn't unusual for boys to shuck a few thousand ears of corn in a day. The competition to see who could do the most ears made fun of the work. It kept the girls busy cutting the kernels from the cob, giving them a quick wash, and we soon heard the golden pebbles plunk into the boiling water.

Huge billows of steam gushed from the boiler, partially escaped out the windows and the remainder crept against the ceiling, down the wall, circled around the kids at the table and diminished into nothingness out the side doors. The day had begun in what soon became an endless process.

The kettle habitually belched forth with the full aroma of new spring corn. The rich, golden smells were quickly pushed into sterilized tin cans, circled under the lid machine and hissed into silence when lowered into the cooling tank. Each can was labeled, pushed into the storage room. We looked for bulges in the can, they meant something was wrong and if stored, the cans would eventually explode.

As I helped store the cans in the warehouse, I read the list of stuff canned the previous year.

825 cans	Asparagus
2773 cans	Sauerkraut
6981 cans	Sweet Corn
2381 cans	Applesauce
380 cans	Pumpkin
5280 cans	Bulk Sauerkraut
4150 cans	String Beans
2298 cans	Beets
1252 quarts	Pickles
7607 cans	Tomato Juice
6135 cans	Tomatoes
125 gallons	Vinegar

The Root Cellar held 5,000 bushels of fruits and vegetables at a constant 38 degrees; equivalent to 10 carload capacities.

Number of pounds of each fresh vegetable to all halls:

114 bunches	Asparagus
130 lbs.	Green Beans
110 lbs.	Beets and Carrots
1500 ears	Corn
100 bunches	Green Onions (15 per bunch)
180 lbs.	Tomatoes
242 lbs.	Grapes
175 lbs.	Rhubarb

The process was always the same each day. Some days I would smell tomatoes all day, others asparagus, carrots; worse of all was sauerkraut; the best were apples and pears. Of course, not everything that came in one door ended up in a can; we ate our share at the cleaning table till we just couldn't stand to chew another bite!

The experience of canning was unforgettable. While working in the hall kitchen someone would often remark, "Hey, you guys, remember when we canned corn last summer?" This was cause for all sorts of comments, recollections of the labor and discontent of giving up a good summer day when we could have been at the lake or swimming in the pool.

There were times when I bowed my head for grace and kept my eyes opened looking at the steaming, hot corn and realized it was snowing outside. The words, "Bless us O Lord and these Thy gifts. . . ." touched a spot within me with deeper understanding and appreciation. The food even tasted better.

I really enjoyed the freedom of wandering around campus without restriction. The watchman was always supervising from his car and this kept me behaving, but I was still Being at the cow barn, petting the calves, poking my finger against the cow's big bag caused me to wonder how what was inside may be in my glass and inside me the next day. I wandered around the barn, read the big sign above the cows:

7 year old . . . in 365 days produced:
26,654 pounds of milk
1,030 pounds butter fat
an average of 71 lbs. milk and 2.82 lbs. butter fat per day

Cows milked and fed three times daily
Feed: corn silage, alfalfa hay, wet beet pulp,
grain ration of 16% protein.

53 pure bred Holstein cows
Average daily: 1,593 pounds of milk 51.6 pounds butter fat.

The first thing I knew I was helping to feed the cows, clean the udders and hook long, rubber hoses to them. The milk left the cow and disappeared into large, shiny cans on the cart, just like the ones delivered to the halls each day.

It wasn't until I was offered a drink of milk that I realized I was supposed to be at the dinner table. I knew this would cost me about ten hours on Special.

Music Appreciation

About once a week we were herded into the auditorium, seated in rows according to classes. In the center of the stage was a large, four-legged radio with the front doors open; the glass lit up as if sending a beacon across the room . . . it was 'music appreciation time.'

"This is Walter Damrosch, bringing you the Symphonic Hour;" and so we sat listening to a broadcast of symphonic music, especially prepared for youth concerts.

It's in situations such as this that adults hope for small miracles and kids are never really aware of the impact of such exposure. As with good art or sculpture, music is not fully appreciated at the moment, but bobs back into one's life at a later date, in a sort of gestation of aesthetics until needed. The weekly appreciation period slowly had its effect and became part of our lives. In my life it didn't bob, it became my life.

"We want our students to know what good music is, whether it be classical, pop or jazz. Jazz certainly has its place in our lives but let it be jazz well rendered. Let us discriminate between good and bad music no matter what kind it is. To do this we must train ourselves and that is the purpose of this music appreciation course. We feel that more benefit is to be derived from this one hour-per-week course than from any course of equal length."

I recall the initial brilliance of sound. I also remember being yelled at by my teacher because, after staring at the large plaster chandeliers overhead, I was bored. I quickly settled down and became occupied staring at the two large stuffed Moose on each side of the stage. I once tried putting my arms around their neck but they were too big. I let go anyway; the eyes seemed to be glaring down at me. Someone said they were real eyes, other guys said they were of glass. They must be glass; one night after band rehearsal I pushed my finger into one eye and it was hard as a rock.

But as time passed, I slowly, but surely, looked forward to the big radio and the wonderful sounds it sent through the auditorium. I learned to hear what was asked of me to hear, the special sounds, combinations of instruments, effects . . . they all made sense and gave great pleasure at the same time.

MY INITIATION INTO MUSIC

I had wandered by the old elementary school portable buildings. Skipping over the log, slat-board walks to the school was always fun; they were very uneven. By jumping just right on the very end of it my weight caused the entire section to rise about five inches and the kid who was chasing me got it right in the middle of his shins and was stopped bone-dead in his tracks. I could see the watchman's car in the distance so I ducked between the portables and crouched down under the window ledge.

Much to my surprise I heard music coming out of the window; the band was playing. They weren't very good; it was the beginning group. I stared through the window a long time, fascinated by all the different horns and what the director was saying. I could see one of my friends blowing a horn. Every now and then he turned the horn upside down, pulled on some tubes and his spit would hit the floor.

I wanted to get his attention so I picked up some small pebbles with my bare toes. With a quick flick from my fingers I shot one like a marble sending the rock through the air and hitting him on the head. He turned, yelled at me. I ducked down past the window ledge before the leader could see me. I couldn't resist the temptation to shoot another pebble into his horn. When he tipped it up I flicked my fingers and the stone made a bulls eye, CLINK, right in the horn.

Before I could shiver, I found myself being dragged through the window, two hands under my armpits. There was plenty of laughing and carrying-on, but all I could see was a red face saying something to me. I was too scared to understand. I was given a chair; a horn just like my friend's. It was shoved into my hands with the threat, "You want to play with a horn, play this." I sat there for quite a while as the band played. Of course, I played around with the slides and even puckered my lips once and pushed them against the mouthpiece. Rehearsal was over. The director looked at me and said,

"You want to join us so badly; I'll see you here for two more days. Understand?" I shook my head in frightened approval.

After all the razzing settled down, I spent an hour in the music room the next day holding this horn, my friend showing me how to hold it and get some sound out. This made me feel good. Besides, I now liked the stuff they were playing.

As the summer progressed I was made a member of the band. My fascination increased; music seemed to flow out of me. I was quickly advanced and within two years I was the youngest kid in the advanced concert band sitting there with seniors and all the biggest boys in school.

Part of my band experience had nothing whatsoever to do with music. There were times when I contributed actions that were not conducive to making good music or pleasant conditions in the band room for other members of the band. Such was the case when I stuffed newspaper into the Tuba. Nothing really happened and I felt perfectly safe . . . until band rehearsal started. The director asked Bill to play his low Bb on the tuba so the band could be tuned. He blew and blew; somewhere in all that air was a muffled Bb, but the director couldn't hear it. All the coaxing in the world caused only a red face and a peck where there should have been a blast! Bill stopped, lifted the tuba over his head and braced it between his legs as it rested on the floor. His hand plunged into the bell and brought out a long trail of newspaper. The laughs around the members of the band ended in a roar. I split my sides as he kept pulling paper out by the hand full. Pretty soon it got quiet and somehow it didn't seem so funny. The director had left the podium and was standing in the middle of the band, which just happened to be next to me. His eyes were glaring and his face was as red as his hair. As he glanced around, his eyes finally rested on me. "And what do you know about this?" I still can't believe he would catch me at first glance. I remember stuttering something in response; the band was laughing. All I could recall was hearing, "200 demerits."

At the cost of 200 demerits I'd be polishing the whole band's shoes for the next parade. The pain stayed with me during the entire rehearsal. How could I work off 200 demerits? This was the last thought I had before dropping off to sleep that night.

It seems that every crisis presents a motivation to overcome the greatest of obstacles; so it was with my demerits. The 200 disturbed me plenty, but it was the 400 demerits I had already accumulated that bothered me. I got those by picking the band room lock so I could practice on Saturday, tieing guys' shoe strings together, knotting ties, exchanging parts of uniforms of short and tall guys, plus lots of other odds and ends that seemed such fun at the time.

During the following rehearsal the director announced that a circus was coming to a nearby town. The top eight members who had the highest number of merits would go with him, at 4:00 in the morning, to see the circus elephants unload from the train. Now, what greater incentive did I need to achieve the impossible? There was much chatter going on, everyone was checking to see how many merits they had. It's funny, but everyone always knew how many merits and demerits they had.

"How'd you like to see the circus?" the director asked me.

"I'd like to." There was laughing from everyone.

"How are you going to work off all your demerits?" There was silence. This answer was not to be missed.

"I could scrub the band room!"

The remarks from all the other guys were thick, but one seemed to penetrate over all the others......With a toothbrush!" This really caused a roar. When the silence came I replied, "With a toothbrush for 400 demerits." The clapping and laughter continued. The director just stood there, our eyes touching as never before. Silence.

"Really?" he asked.

"Really," I replied. I kept my eyes on him. I could sense the others looking at both of us, first at one then at the other. I knew he was truly searching for the answer; I had learned to hold him with more respect than the other teachers.

He said, "Okay." I kept staring at him, our eyes kept contact. I had grown a little more in a way as never before, yet no words were said. I was suddenly jolted into reality by the thunderous whistling, clapping and yelling. I looked toward the podium and saw his friendly smile. I knew I was going to the circus.

To scrub the band room, four practice rooms and storage area took almost eight hours and four toothbrushes. After polishing tubas, band trophies and almost every pair of shoes of the band members the demerit total disappeared and a few merits began to register on my record. It seems I not only had the knack for demerits but a real talent for doing odd jobs that produced merits by 5, 10 and 25 points each.

Joy came by basket fulls for me as I stood by the railroad to watch 16 lumbering elephants within 10 feet of me. My world literally stopped. It wasn't until the circus was over and we were going home when someone asked, "I wonder how long it would take to scrub an elephant with a toothbrush?" I laughed and the director laughed. We just looked at each other.

∾

CONCERT STAGE

Every Sunday the steam whistle blew at 3:00 and the auditorium seemed to devour the entire student body and regurgitate them in an hour or so. Almost everyone belonged to the band, orchestra, mixed chorus or some musical organization. It was not unusual for kids to belong to three or four groups; some were on the stage performing 50 out of 52 Sundays during the entire year. When the big combined concerts were given, sometimes there were only 150 kids in the audience, the rest were visitors.

The concerts were the culmination of some phase of perfection by a specific group; concert band, orchestra, one of the many choirs, dance band or a single performance as pipe organ soloist. Daily broadcasts through the radio station came from the stage. Our groups had many champions, winning first place in district and state contests, plus many national contests.

As with most offerings at school the membership in musical organizations were open to everyone. At one time almost 1,000 students of the 1,500 participated in music

organizations of one kind or another. No credit was given on
school records for this.

It was motivation that was responsible. This one element
pervaded the sports and other activities and made Mooseheart
a school of champions.

To practice an hour every day on one's own made our
groups the best. The repertoires of concerts were in classifica-
tions far in excess of our rating according to our chronological
ages. Within these groups we met the finest classics and were
taught by instructors who were determined above all else to
inspire ... to perform was natural ... to grow and be changed
by these performances was something no other medium could
instill. Having pride made us proud.

The band traveled to Canada. Our new uniforms didn't
arrive until the day we left for the trip. Frustration was rampant
because pant legs were too long, coat sleeves fell over our
hands and we were barely able to play. Straight pins, belts
tightened to hold up baggy seats and safety pins to last until
we got home to the tailor, soon remedied all this.

It is difficult to recall any one time when there was a
feeling of defeat or a pessimistic attitude in the groups. It was
just understood that we would practice hard, get it perfect,
perform our very best and that's it. Our life was Mooseheart
and whatever Mooseheart was, so were we.

My instructors told me that there is a direct relationship
between those who practice hours on an instrument and their
individual academic achievement. It takes discipline to dig
into a new subject, work it through and then expect to perform
it. This discipline also permeated the fundamentals of our
success as a group; everyone was success oriented.

We performed most of the Gilbert and Sullivan works; they were humorous, had lots of good solo parts and the chorus was active. The social development in an activity of this type is inestimable. As with any performances, the participants are more closely bound afterwards.

Each year we performed the "Messiah." This masterpiece developed our spiritual sensitivity to such an extent that it acted as religious training for us. I played organ for a few of the choruses and solos.

And, so it was; solo and ensemble contests, choirs, band and orchestras, dance band, marching band, music, music, music.... I became a sensitive being.

EXCHANGE ASSEMBLY - PIANO

Before music entered my life, it seemed to be in bits and pieces. Then, all of a sudden everything made sense. I was always busy; involved in so many things that just being involved was the most important thing to me.

What I was learning and how it fit into what adults called the "whole picture" took a long time for me to understand. Learning to play the piano and the French Horn, singing in the choirs, being captain of the soccer team were important to me simply for the doing. I had no final idea of how this was all to come together to me, as a person.

As I grew older I participated in contests and other public performances. I was realizing I was alone on the stage doing more and more things by myself. I felt good about this, enjoyed the doing and looked forward to these moments despite the fact I could only fall back upon myself to do what was being done. The me, in me, felt very happy.

A happening in my life at the exchange assembly, which was performed at a large neighboring school in Joliet, brought all these feelings into focus. I was first on the program, playing a piano solo. The stage was twice our size, the audience so big I could not see the back of the balcony. As I walked on the stage the applause was very unexpected; I hadn't even played yet. The volume overpowered me and I became very excited.

The piano was isolated in stage-center. As I prepared to sit down I noticed the puffy, shiny-leather bench with one knob on each side. Seated, I was now aware the top of the grand piano was slanted up and it was the longest stringed piano I had ever seen. Nothing like the uprights I practiced on in the practice rooms. I was scared; I got up and ran back-stage. The laughing from the audience didn't bother me as much as that giant piano.

After some explanation and clarification from my teacher I was seated and playing with the knobs on the seat, going up and down till I felt the right height. The audience became very quiet. I looked across the miles of strings and as I hit the first chord of Beethoven's "Sonata Pathetique." I was struck with the magnificence of the luscious, sound of the piano. I could see the strings shiver up and down in a vibration so powerful that I wanted this sound to fulfill a swelling need within me. I was above wherever I had been before and I was extremely happy. The more I played, the more everything jelled into an exhilaration I had never felt before. I wanted to play forever. The final chord resounded and the audience returned to me a thunderous applause. I touched the piano with a caress knowing somehow that I, too, had been touched in a way that was very precious.

My teacher hugged me with, "That was the best you've ever played; absolutely great." I returned to face the audience alone and gave a bow to them in gratefulness, thanking them deep inside myself for such a supreme moment.

Autumn–Winter

Autumn was walnuts, winter pears, pumpkins and rabbit-shagging time. Those darn walnuts were always a problem. On the trees they were covered with a hard, green shell. When they fell, or we spent half a day almost breaking our necks climbing trees and stomping on branches shaking them to the ground, they were wrinkled and brown. Autumn might be called the 'brown skin season,' because as we cracked the skin of the nut this awful, brown stain oozed out. It didn't matter what we did; once the stain got on our hands or under our fingernails, soap, lye, sand scrubbing . . . nothing gets it off but time. It seemed like one day every kid in school had clean, white nails and over the weekend every kid came to school with brown-dyed hands.

Trying to hide our sacks full of walnuts was more bother than the brown stain. We had to bury the nuts so they would dry-out. We would walk around the lake trying to ditch everybody, dig a hole, mark it in a secret way and then walk away fast. Six weeks later we'd dig them up, get two big rocks and spend half a day banging away, cracking shells for the good stuff inside. It was worth every sore finger.

The turning of the autumn leaves did something to my spirit that nothing else ever could. All the spiritual instruction I received changed from words and found form in nature. There was no other experience that could replace walking in the woods seeing leaves spiraling to the ground, gently falling on my head. One day the trees were full of green, then gradually yellow, rust, gold and brown, . . . all trees finally standing barren, naked against the cold sky. It was something I lived; it was something that changed me. It became me.

Just as in the spring, when small clumps of green burst forth, I seemed to be singing a hymn to the woods as I realized I had come full circle inside myself.

WINTER

Winter was very special to me. As a boy it meant slipping on frozen puddles, sloshing through snow, making snowballs and having snowball fights, making a snowman and climbing onto his shoulders. Winter was something I got into; I ran into the wind and pushed myself into the thickness of the new drifts.

Now that I am older I let the winter get into me. There is majesty in the falling of snow, the way the flakes float on the nothingness of the slightest wind, twirling in their dance. How softly they touch my cheek, to melt as a tear in the warmth of our meeting.

I would look upwards into the darkening sky to see this creation of beauty as if it were dropping from invisible hands. The chill does not shake my body but invigorates me, stirs me into an exhilaration of the magic of the moment. And within the stillness there is yet so much movement.

I would question the crunch of my footsteps, contrasting this sound to the sounds of the wind through the trees. I thought deeply about how sounds were made. These were the sounds of winter.

The thing I enjoyed most was walking to band rehearsal in the dark of night after supper. The fields were like a pure newly laundered white sheet, an endless crest of new-fallen snow. The light of the full moon shadowed the drifts. Trees were frozen in silhouette against the sky, casting their shadows through the shimmering flakes. I looked back into the sunken footprints and saw black holes punctuating where I had been, like records of a life that were moving forward. All of this made a difference: I felt like a different person, as I looked ahead, different from the person looking back.

Snowflakes buzzed 'round the lighted lamppost, just like the bugs during a hot summer evening. All the lights seemed to be floating in a stream leading to the auditorium. I followed it, excited to be in rehearsal.

After the rehearsal I was tired. The giving of myself during rehearsal always drained me in a way that left me oddly excited.

The walk home was beautiful, quiet. The moon had changed position. New shapes and shadows occupied my sight. As I reached my hall, I took one last look at the incredible picture framed in the doorway. The paint was hardly dry on the picture I carried in my heart.

∾

CHRISTMAS

Long before the Christmas chimes rang and cut through the quiet of a snowy evening I sat in an easy chair in the dayroom to read over the Christmas list available to all the kids. I could choose whatever gift I wanted: ice-skates, tie clasp set, roller skates, puzzles, pen-pencil set; it was a long list of choices. The decision to pick out a gift for myself was something I did not get to do very often. It was for me, not exactly from me, but sort of from me because I was doing the choosing. My thoughts filtered through my desires, picturing how I would use roller skates when the snow melted, how I would feel dressed-up with the tie clasp set. Christmas was a long way off, and it was hard to feel Christmassy without the smell of the tree, the sound of carols and being let out of school.

I talked to a group of other kids and we all naturally wanted everything on the list. I finally completed my slip. Even after I turned it in, my mind kept picking other things.

No kid at Mooseheart ever went without a gift of some sort. There was always something under the tree with his name on it. It may not have been what he wanted but there were always other kids who wanted to trade what they got; that evened things out.

I particularly liked the sound of Christmas. Practicing carols in the choir and preparing for the programs meant more to me than the gifts. Maybe it was the words, reflecting what they mean now and meant in the days past. I often thought the words themselves were gifts, gifts that I received and could only give to another person through singing.

Being with the band stirred me into a happy mood, full of rhythm and different feelings, yet, still Christmas. There's something about trumpets and flutes that go with shouting the joy of the season. The orchestra was another matter. The strings smoothed out my thoughts and filtered into the warmth that flooded the Christmas crèche. This was okay by me.

The Christmas church services were the best of the entire holiday feast for me. Everyone sang better, everything sounded better, the whole feeling, sight, and smell brought the everything of Christmas together. The praying was like having your prayers answered while you said them. I knew then there was a Jesus. He was really there. There was nothing around to say He wasn't and everything to say He was.

SLEDDING AND SKATING

I could always tell when sledding and ice skating season was upon us. In the morning the windows looked like fractured glass and water puddles reflected like mirrors.

It was hard to judge the winter days at first because it would start out cold and by noon I would be sweating. This didn't last very long; the matron would soon have all my summer pants and short-sleeve shirts packed away. All I could find now were long shirts, long pants, long gloves, and long underwear, everything long; winter was definitely here.

It was only natural that we headed toward the lake. Sometimes there was a line a mile long of kids wrapped up looking like penguins headed in that one direction.

The lucky guys had a sled. If I was lucky I had a friend who said he'd share his for the day. If I were not lucky at all I'd head for the dump, find a board and use that. If I were downright unlucky, I'd slide down hills all day on my rear end.

The best hill in the school was the one leading down to the dam. It's almost straight down. We'd spend hours tromping up and down the hill to get the snow packed tight. There were always two slides, each about equal to the car tracks worn into the road. Two boys could use the hill at once and not get hurt. The guy who was the fastest would always go over the dam road and spillway without any trouble.

The more the hill was packed the slicker it became and the faster we could travel. Later on we got the idea of pouring water on the hill, letting it freeze over-night so we could go a hundred miles an hour. We soon formed a brigade, going in and out of the rear door of a nearby hall, lugging buckets, boxes, cups, whatever would hold water.

It was the sloppiest mess you ever saw. Boys began to look like icemen from the water they spilled over themselves. The hill finally did get covered. We left with an elated sense of accomplishment knowing nature would freeze it slick as a mirror.

The next day we could hardly wait; we shot down to the hill right after school. There we stood, about 50 of us; all lined up like crows on a fence, looking down on the sorriest, stony road we ever saw. The sun was out bright and full, water trickling down the gutters, over the rocks, joining the rest of the snow and ice on its way to the river. Undaunted, we tried again and this time it worked. ICE, slick as glass. We had manufactured our own brand of heaven-on-earth.

Very few kids owned ice skates so we would slant our feet inward so the outside heavy part of our shoe sole would act as an ice skate blade. Once this caught on, every kid in school had to try it. I skated this way for years. Going down the hill this way was a thrill I could never forget. The shoemaker would throw up his hands when he would get dozens of pairs of shoes with the outside soles worn away and the rest of the shoe in almost perfect condition. Everyone literally wore their 'skates' everywhere they went. Small frozen puddles, packed snow paths, sidewalks with a film of ice; all served as an excuse to flip feet on the side and skate.

When the red flag flew at the top of the flagpole by the American Flag it was skating day at the lake. All the precautions of keeping off the ice until it was frozen thick enough for skating were soon resolved. The coaching staff chopped a hole to determine if it was 1½ to 2 feet thick, safe for skating. Just to be certain, farmhands led four huge, plough horses on the ice, circled around the lake and came back. The coach yelled, "Skate," and ten times the weight of the horses clamored on the ice and slithered around like woolen clothed beetles.

Our favorite was 'Crack-the-Whip.' About 50 kids assembled at the steel cables by the creek and started the slow snake-like trail down toward the dam. It was my first time at the end of the whip ... I was going to be 'cracked.' All misfortune was mine. I had borrowed clamp-on skates, too big, one broken shoe string and still in the wobbly-ankles stage of skating. I was at the end of the line ready to be 'whipped.' Yells of "Whip" traveled down the line and all arms strained to hold the chain together. I could feel my speed increase. My feet had long stopped trying to skate; my ankles increased their wobbling.

Out of the corner of my eye I could see the log cabin on shore disappear and at the same moment the hand I was gripping so tightly opened; I found myself all alone. The wind whistled past my head, blew off my stocking cap, my arms swung through the air in a million gyrations as I tried to keep my balance. None of this seemed to matter so much as my concern that I must be going at least a hundred miles an hour.

What I thought was a long distance to the dam suddenly seemed to be right in front of me. In pure desperation of visualizing myself flying over the dam standing straight up, I took a nose-dive onto the ice. I remember snow spewing over me, my body turning `round and `round, arms spread like a rabbit on a crotch at the dump, eventually coming to a stop. I couldn't move; I was sure I was dead. A numbness crept over my entire body. I closed my eyes.

"Don't move; don't move." I thought I was dreaming, but the voice repeated again, "Don't move, don't move." I opened my eyes and some distance in front of me was the coach. "Just don't move, stay where you are. Grab this rope. Hold tight." I did as he said. I could feel myself being pulled over a ledge. He grabbed my hands and I felt somewhat secure. I had spun in a circle on the ice, miraculously coming to rest with my feet and legs floating in the icy water just a few feet from the top of the dam. I was taken to the hospital and checked out okay. The rules for "Cracking-the-Whip" were slightly changed; **'FACE CREEK FOR CRACK-THE-WHIP.'**

∾

The Inner Search

Every gentile kid at Mooseheart spent at least one hour per week in religious instruction with the Catholic priest or the Protestant minister. The Jewish kids went off campus for their instruction and church services.

These were the serious classes. First of all, I was dealing with God and the priest represented God. Secondly, this religious instruction served to further bind the entire school together making all us kids one family with a father at the head. What was taught seemed to be special, related to all the other things we learned in school and helped give meaning to the many swarming loose ends of our lives as orphans.

Church was no chore to me. I enjoyed being alone with my own thoughts. As I delved into the mysteries of my being, my relationship with a higher power became part of the quest. I had to search all the unknown questions of my existence. That I could have power through faith in itself was a mystery to me and I wanted to nourish this concept so that it would be a source of strength as much as food was to my body.

CHAPEL

Before we had the new church, as it stands now, I celebrated my faith in the auditorium. The oak seats we used
Saturday night for movies on the stage were turned in the
opposite direction to face the altar and the organ. This building
was used for every large meeting; school assemblies, Moose
Lodge, graduation, school dances, because it had a wooden
floor; you name it, it served a thousand purposes. It held the
entire school population.

It wasn't until I helped to clean the priest's house that I
had my deepest feeling of spirituality. In it was a small chapel
for Father Laffey to say his daily Mass and special occasions.
Many times I opened the door and hesitated to go in, but
finally ended up in the absolute silence with only myself. The
burning, red candle to let me know I was in the presence of
holiness. Sometimes I prayed. Mostly I sat there looking at
the candle, the flame so straight, not a breeze to make it flicker.
The gold altar cloth with its lacy edges gave me the feeling of
how delicate I could feel, how small things impressed me,
how things just seemed to be held together by such small
contacts.

The way the chapel was built pleased me. The scrolls,
small columns, the chalice, all blended into an impression
that this was the correct way of living. It was a beauty to carry
with me, a way to be in my everyday life. My prayers seemed
to mean more when I sat so close to the altar; it became part
of me. That I was, in fact, more than just me at this moment
was as true as anything I had ever known.

When I left the chapel I was concerned that I did not

slam the door, even checking it to make sure it was shut, as though the inside could escape if I left it opened. Somehow I wanted what was there to be there when I returned. I had it in me, but I knew it was still there, too.

HOUSE OF GOD

I could not believe my eyes when I first saw the walls of the new church being built. It was also the first time I had seen any building being built from the ground up. The wide open spaces between the pillars seemed gigantic, like the great walls I recalled seeing in magazines about churches in Europe. The huge granite blocks that made the outside walls assured me it would last forever. The spaces for windows were left open and it wasn't until the stained glass was installed that a warmth and closed-in feeling gave me the assurance that God would enter and stay within.

The arches meant freedom and security. The ornate corners crowned the majesty of this great building. The shafts of light reflected through the colored windows, softened the pews and marble floor. The eye of my soul had never seen so much before and I had feelings I did not know existed.

Some kids ran to church. Others took their time, assured that God was there. I always sat in the church pew closest to the stained glass window depicting the good Shepherd and the sheep. The colors were so vivid, the blue cloak, blue eyes. The beard of the Shepherd was soft, long and curled and the wooden staff appealed to the potential spirit within me. The sheep were woolly, grazing, some looking at Christ and others spread over the distant hill. The children knelt on the wooden kneeler, their hands clasped close together, their fingers curled one over the other as though keeping their thoughts and body entwined in their closeness to God. Others leaned to the side watching the flickering altar candles.

My eyes continued to follow from one stained glass picture to another, staring, moving and absorbing the meaning of the scene and story as well as the light. I traced the thick pillar to the ceiling, amazed at how the arch can be suspended. How did it hold itself in place?

The sermon was always fulfilling. My troubles disappeared as I heard comforting words, stories of Christ and good things that happened to people. My thoughts would often float around like a gull over water, and then some new phrase spoken by the priest would again bring me back to church. I stared at the pulpit. The priest was my confessor, my friend, a man who knew more about me and my thoughts than any other person. I could tell him the things I thought about, things only he and I would ever know about me. It was only right that this was so; he guided my soul and I trusted him. His words affected my thinking. Where there was confusion he explained it away. I often wondered what I would be like if these changes had not taken place within me. I knew I was different after being in church. Even though I changed my Sunday clothes to everyday clothes, I still felt this difference.

With the Catholic priest, the Protestant minister, Reverend Paine, received equally high respect of everyone and was much sought after for his wisdom. Between these two men of God, the welfare, spirituality and morality, of all students remained at a proud level befitting human dignity.

After using the auditorium as a church for so many years this new church was an experience that was never to leave my mind. The church was only for church, for God; not for dances, assemblies, rehearsals and programs. Every time I entered I had the same feeling of being taken from myself; and being absorbed by the strength of the walls, the lifting of the arches and the beauty of the stained glass windows.

My life was at last blessed with peace and quiet.

Mothers

All children came to Mooseheart because of the death of their father. There is probably nothing with a more traumatic impact for a loving mother than to know or realize that she will have to live separately from any of her living children, especially when they are only across the street. To enter Mooseheart was the most crucial decision she must have ever made. Many questions must have been answered within her heart before she consented to such a situation.

Our father had been killed in an automobile accident late at night, with no witnesses. The family was left destitute, relying upon relatives to support them. Members of the family had suggested our mother take the family to Mooseheart; our life would be much better, the family would supposedly be together. And, the official who came from Mooseheart assured her future would be safe and that we would all get the best of possible care without worry to her. She was afraid we would be separated and she would not be able to be with us at all. She was assured she would be able to visit us but that we'd be in different homes according to our ages and supervised by other 'mothers' who also had children there. She was assured she would be assigned to taking care of other children. This eased her mind. She was convinced in so many ways that her five boys would be taken care of that she finally consented.

She recalls how surprised she was to see the different buildings, baby village, the doctor's to take care of the sick children, a big hospital, grass and trees, a beautiful lake and flowers over the entire grounds. When she understood the care and discipline that would be given her sons she decided that we should be taken care of in this place. Years later she remarked, "Giving my consent was the best decision I ever made."

Most of the matrons, or housemothers, were women who had children of their own at Mooseheart. My own mother often remarked, "How very difficult it was for all of them to have charge of 30 kids, none of whom were their own flesh and blood."

Our mother had free time off each week to visit and spend time with us, as she wanted. Of course, she attended all our programs and movies. There was a special Women's Club that all the mothers shared. She was more than an employee; she had a personal interest in the welfare and education of those she cared for.

For her not to be in the hall with her children was based on the premise that it would give unfair advantage to her own children. Children are not as charitable to each other's short-comings or eccentricities as are adults. There is a tendency for other kids to feel the natural mother is giving special favors to her own child. It was difficult to remain neutral and impartial.

My Mom was first assigned to a hall with another matron until she learned more of Mooseheart and became adjusted to its ways. She was a master seamstress and was later assigned to the sewing department, making clothes needed for the hundreds of kids at the school. It was difficult for her to drop in and see us, her own children. Her maternal needs made her want to reach out to us. We did not receive the casual hugs when we wanted them.

It was the matron who was the godsend to the kids in her charge. She somehow miraculously answered this cry for a mother, coming from 30 children.

It was traumatic to be with one housemother and then be transferred to another hall and have to get acquainted with a new housemother and new kids. This was inevitable as Mooseheart was set up so similar age groups were housed together and located next to one another.

Where other kids in life remember fathers, mothers and teachers, Mooseheart kids remember teachers, matrons, cooks and watchmen. If I was asked, "How was your Dad?" I replied, "He died when I was such and such an age."

When asked, "How was your Mom?" I knew I had a Mom and loved her, but I had a group of housemothers, too, that I also loved.

MOTHER'S DAY

Mother's Day was a special day at Mooseheart. It was usually celebrated on a Sunday. Every kid who had a mother there wore a red carnation; the others wore a white one. We five brothers went to church with our Mother as a family.

It wasn't until I was older that the red and white difference in the flowers first signified a sense of family value to me. I was so busy leading the life I was living that it took a special occasion such as this to give it meaning.

Mother's Day was the one day our Mom ate with us at the same table in the same hall; the whole family was together for the first time since we could remember. I hardly knew what to say to my brothers because I was so used to eating with my usual hall-mates. It was the one time I felt the sense that Mothers and families are related in a close unit, even though we took each other for granted. It was also the first time I deeply felt my mother physically leaving us when she walked out the door and had to go to another hall where she lived.

The feeling was new and strange and left me empty. I was also sensitive, for the first time that other boys didn't have any Mom to eat with them or leave them. I couldn't exactly know how they felt. It was very mysterious.

The people who were my proctors, matrons, cooks, teachers, priest and minister eventually became an essence of my very being. What they said, how they said it, how they acted, reacted; their impact upon me as individuals, and how they handled me became a large part of me. Where other children go home to parents, a few brothers or sisters, then to school and mingle with hundred of different kids in a different social situation, I did not. I was part of a close, thirty-member small-knit family, sometimes living with the same kids for three, maybe five years or longer.

A total of some thousand kids passed one another each day. We frequently were in the same dorm, classroom, work detail, choir, dining table, etc., with the same few people or with one particular individual as though glued together.

Our 'family' of friends were the same as brothers and sisters all day, all week, all year. We lived closer together in everything we did than most families in actual life situations. And, we came from all over the country. Our ages were about the same but that's all we had in common. Certainly, our parents and family background must have been as diverse as the number of leaves on the trees at the lake. Yet, with all this diversity we somehow became a cohesive unit and were soon recognized as 'the kids from Mooseheart.'

MEMORIAL DAY

Memorial Day was always a very special event. The band marched and played hymns and music I had never heard them play before. Everything was so quiet. As we walked through the campus, the kids were different; there was no scuffing of feet or kicking of stones. It was hot.

With so many bodies close together the breeze from the lake hardly had time to cool us. I stared at the nursery, wondering how rabbit-shagging would be this fall. A quail flew up; I knew she had eggs on a nest. The lake was very still.

As we neared the cemetery the band played "Nearer My God To Thee." We were told to go inside the chain that circled the cemetery but no one wanted to sit next to the gravestones.

The Protestant chaplain pronounced the prayer and all heads bowed in reverence. A stranger in uniform started a speech but I didn't understand much of what he was saying. It just seemed to be getting hotter and hotter. My mind wandered a lot; watching birds, trying to see the lake.

I began looking at the gravestones, wondering who was buried there. I could read about eight of them. The last one really made me think. I read the last name of one of my friends. How did his name get there? It said something about 1923-1927. That's only four years. That must have been his baby sister he said he had. I was very upset just knowing someone whose family was actually buried here at Mooseheart. I always thought kids came here, stayed and finally graduated and left; nobody ever died.

The trumpet player stood by the gravestones and slowly played the first part of 'Taps.' From way across the lake came an echo played by another guy from the band. This moment of silence settled us.

We all had to stand while the Catholic priest gave the closing prayer. When he said, "Let us remember those who have left us," I felt very different inside. I realized that I knew someone who had lost someone forever.

The walk home was slow. It seemed I looked at the lake all the time but my mind was far, far away, tossing in thoughts I never thought before.

Boys ... Girls ... Love

It did not take an earth-shattering experience for a boy to like a girl! It was a simple act; just write a note to a girl and ask, "Will you go with me?" When you felt good with a girl and shared lots of talk and got along well, you just asked her the question. Sometimes your friends told you some girl really liked you and wanted to go with you and that made it easier, but you still had to ask. The answer was almost always, "Yes."

You didn't mind a "No" too much, unless the girl went with another guy you didn't like. If that was the case you thought it was crummy of her to do a thing like that to you. How could she possible turn you down for some dumb guy like him?

Finding my place with a girl was always a bit bewildering. Now that we're going together what do we talk about? Sometimes a boy's behavior changes and he feels he has to put on his extra good manners; otherwise she will leave him.

Going together was an 'it depends feeling'. If you want to kiss a girl, 'it depends' on if she wants to be kissed; the same thing for holding hands. It was okay when you're by yourselves, but when you were walking out on campus or to school and you saw an old boyfriend coming or your best friends who might make some snotty comment to you, well, that was a different story. You soon find out that you've sort of had it, like when you want to drop her hand and she squeezes yours and you can't let go. You just let it hang limp, as though you really don't care and you think the other guys will see you're not squeezing. Of course, she could put her other hand on your arm and snuggle close to you while squeezing your hand off. No matter what you think, you're dead. There's just no other way the other guys could think; you smile, she smiles and the snotty comments can't separate you.

It wasn't long and your girl was off limits to other guys. "Oh, she goes with John, you better not monkey around with her!" Some guys and girls went together for years. If they broke up it was a traumatic experience. There was crying, writing notes, trying to make up, standing in the school hallway 'till the last second hoping to see her; being tardy to class and getting low grades. Your mind just couldn't settle down.

It's not the mind really, but the feelings that were hurt, and that's something you can't get your mind to figure out. It is important, however, that the feelings feel.

When it was all over and you found yourself still breathing and you could eat and shoot your slingshot, you know you were okay. The real test was to pass her on the street or in school and say "Hi" to one another, just testing out the relationship. Once this was done everything seemed to settle down and you were back eating second helpings of mash potatoes and gravy at the next meal. In two weeks there was another girl holding your hand and you were going down the same road again.

When I was a senior in school I was really serious about Leila. There was something about holding her hand that just did not stop the squeezing through the rest of me. I felt warm inside, everything about me seemed to be going very fast; I was anxious and charged, as if hooked to a dynamo.

The day started with anticipation of seeing her. She kept popping into my thoughts as I did my dishwashing assignments in the hall; she was becoming ever present in everything I did. As soon as the whistle blew for us to leave the hall and go to school I was at the front door chomping-at-the-bit, ready to clear the steps and run.

I would meet her on the curb of the girls' campus. That gave us more time and distance to walk together. Although I was pooped out from running I acted like it was only a short walk. The muscles in my legs jiggled and my feet could hardly take the slow pace. Our hands met and the first squeeze of the day put everything in good order.

My first love made me aware of how much I like to look at a girl, her eyes, and nose, how soft her lips were. Kissing was out of the question; it just wasn't done until you knew each other better. It wasn't that I didn't think about it, 'cause I did; there was just so much else happening inside of me I didn't have the time to figure out how I would kiss a girl.

Being close to her soon made me aware that she had a smell about her that I liked; it was different from guys. I always thought it was a girl smell, sweet. When she leaned her head on my shoulder or touched her hand to my chest I could feel this closeness and I was affected as I never had been before. It was special and was only for me.

I had never shared this kind of feeling before and I felt

something from inside me reach out and grab it; I enjoyed it and didn't want to lose it. Lots of things soon became accepted between us and our freedom to share, touch and accept what the other gave was part of 'us.'

We looked forward to Sunday when the whistle blew and the boys could go on the girls' campus. I don't recall ever making plans where to meet, we just seemed to be there together as if prearranged.

During the week we talked across the road that separated boys and girls campus. The rule was 'boys . . . at least one foot on your own curb, the girls on their own sidewalk.' I reckon every boy spent a couple of thousand hours with one foot on the curb and the other in the gutter tromping his way back and forth between the Campanile Tower and Erie Hall.

Walking on the girls campus was fun. Although we were told to stay on the sidewalks all the time, there were plenty of bushes and trees around which sidewalks very nicely wandered and curved around.

Our chaperon couldn't be everywhere and see everything. She was a mother assigned to patrol the girls campus during visiting hours. It was one of those jobs that no matter who had it, even my own mother, she would not be liked. It detracted from our few hours of liberty with our girlfriends; in our eyes, she was a spy.

I spent lots of time behind the flagpole trees and Aid Hall bushes sharing a quick kiss or trying to get my arm around Leila. I got caught once. I guess I underestimated the chaperone's speed. She must have taken a shortcut across the grass, but God, there she was. I had my arms around Leila's waist, our lips touching, my eyes closed.

"Now, you don't want to do that, do you?" she asked.

It's kind of hard to say what my feelings were. How do you stop kissing your girl, try to act like nothing was happening and at the same time give the old bag the idea you knew she was coming and you weren't surprised at all and still keep your voice from shaking and stuttering? Worst of all, it put my girl in the frame of mind that we better not try this again or we'll get caught; that just didn't set right with me.

I got five hours on special assignment. The worst part was I had to serve the time on the next Sunday, just when the whistle blew for everyone to visit their girls on girls' campus. It was a bummer.

Instruction in sex was not part of our school curriculum and was left to the religious leaders as part of our instruction. I was Catholic, so the priest gave me what lessons I got. I never thought too much about kissing girls; I wanted to kiss them, but this moral training set boundaries and conditions, which served to guide me in my actions. Touch them? Never.

I heard words such as pregnant, but this was a mystery as to what it meant. One boy told me kissing did it. Another said, "If you hug too close, you've had it." The priest spoke of girls' legs, how we were not to look under skirts and see above the stockings, but I never knew what was above the stocking anyway.

Being with a Mooseheart girl was good. I felt we were the same, the same feelings, the same thoughts; my worries of all the other unknown things were far away from everything I knew. It was just understood that holding hands, kissing, hugging, were things you did with your girlfriend. The other thoughts somehow got into my head but that's as far as they got; there was always my upbringing, religion, rules and regulations that barricaded the next unknown action. I knew I could love a girl and she could love me and kissing was our way of expressing it most profoundly.

∾

The Beginning of Maturity

My late teen life was productive, involved with activities and lacking in conflict. If there was a conflict it was the concern for whom I was and what I wanted to do for a living. I was becoming aware that I would be leaving Mooseheart, my meals would not be waiting for me on the table and I would have to purchase my own clothes. The world outside would not take care of me; I would have to care for myself. How was this done? Getting money was not a concern in my growing up process for I never needed money.

My satisfaction with myself, and what I was doing that made me feel good about myself, was due to a large degree to the success I was having in music. I was the best in this endeavor, challenged by others with the same drive for success. There were always older kids who were doing things I admired. I also knew, and saw that success was based upon a person giving of himself in order to gain this success. Practicing to perfection for performances and gaining this discipline was part of every success; if I were to have what I wanted, this attitude had to go with it. I never felt otherwise.

I knew almost everyone in school by first name; all the way from first grade through 12th grade.

The strength of my own identity was there, even though I continued to question the future. I seemed to know and somehow feel that deep down inside I had whatever I needed to survive and to come out on top. I never thought of failure. I didn't think that way; I wasn't acquainted with it.

My whole life had been competition with each new game or musical number I attempted. There were approaches to new endeavors constantly. I pulled myself through all the challenges and there were no doubts that the efforts were stronger than the problems. Resistance and doubt were there, but the other disciplines and desires always overpowered them.

I noticed this growing confidence in myself when I went to music contests away from my school at district, state and national contests. I was always aware of how good other kids were, how tremendous was their talent and ability. I sat listening to them with doubts in my mind as to my ability comparing what they could do, wanting to be able to play as well as they did. I knew so well what it took to be that good.

Each time when my turn came I did not doubt myself. I knew that what I knew was deep within me. I knew this through the strength of other performances, my teacher's encouragements and all my successes that overpowered the several failures. There was a sense of greatness in what I was doing, the music I was performing; I had worked so hard for all of this.

I won again and again and again. Doubt had always been present somewhere in my doing but never to the point where it would stop me. There were times when it was present and its very being there would become the reason for conquering it. Failures became successes, which led to the next step, the next challenge. I liked loving music and I liked myself.

ENTER TO LEARN-LEAVE TO SERVE

At the entrance of Mooseheart was a stone inscription that read: 'ENTER TO LEARN ... LEAVE TO SERVE.' I never quite understood this because I never thought I was entering. I was there. 'Leave to Serve' was a mystery; leaving was not a concept in my mind. This place was my home. I accepted everything from the entrance sign to the creek at the lake as the place where I lived. It was only as I grew older that the word, 'leave' came into focus and gave meaning to the statement.

Then one day my being in The Child City took on greater meaning and understanding. I read some literature that stated simply, 'All children will receive an education and a trade, be clothed and nourished and trained to be men and women of character.'

I never thought about character. I doubt if any kid did. Yes, we had called each other "characters" in the way one calls each other 'crazy.' But any other thought of the word was not part of us. We were just kids getting into trouble and serving hours and hours on special assignment, going to church and playing in the band, orchestra, singing in choirs, going to school, doing our assignments. I wondered what all this had to do with being trained to be men and women of character.

GRADUATION

Commencement at The Child City is different. There are no fathers, only a scattering of mothers. The great majority of the kids are double orphans. No father sits quietly renewing plans for the future of his son who at this moment is reaching for his diploma. And, of the mothers, few, if any, are charting a profession or a place in society or in the home. This IS their home.

We orphans, upon leaving our Alma Mater, faced a world largely on our own. We left our school, our home really, not to fill places already prepared for us by devoted parents, but through our own efforts to create places for ourselves. We faced the inevitable strivings, anxieties, and disappointments and the successes alone.

The day of my graduation the orchestra filled the music pit and with the first blast of Bach's "March Noble" the high school principal entered the door to the Auditorium. The priest delivered the invocation and related our life to the future. Hearing the Father's voice that day and knowing I would not hear it again was a great personal sorrow. He asked his blessings upon us and our unseen needs. The words seemed to weigh more importantly than any lesson ever presented in my school classes.

Each occasion to sing our school song proved to be a

slow process of giving ourselves to its ideals, a way of life and living with others, a weaving in and out of the thread of our common needs until we were of the same fabric.

With the final realization this was the last day I would be here, secluded and sheltered and must abruptly face the uncertain future, I did not find this to be the happiest moment of my life. I would not be here, not again, not ever. What had been the words of that day now became questions, wonderings and speculations on my growth in this life I had known. I knew then I would never be able to separate it from my life as long as I would live. All our anguishes and happiness's were one. We were inseparable.

My thoughts suddenly stopped when I heard them announce that a French horn solo was to be played. My friend had been a National Contest winner, just like me; I had been with him in the horn quartet. This was the same year The Child City had sent 40 State Winners to the National Contest with a return of 24 National Winners. It was some sort of record. I had established a record, also, for I was the first child to ever win in four separate categories at a National Contest: French Horn solo, Piano solo, Student Conducting, French Horn Quartet.

༒

JAMES J. DAVIS, FOUNDER OF MOOSEHEART

The graduating class wasn't very big so it didn't take long to give out the diplomas. My name was called. I went to the stage, shook hands with the founder of The Child City, and took the paper in my other hand. His handshake was firm and his eyes said things I never understood. I was standing in the presence of greatness, a dreamer of men, as living proof of the fulfillment of his dream.

The founder of Mooseheart set one of the creeds of the City of Children, as our home was called. 'EVERY CHILD IS ENTI-TLED TO A HIGH SCHOOL EDUCATION AND TRAINING IN A VOCATION FITTING HIM FOR LIFE'S WORK.'

James J. Davis gave the commencement speech.

"You do not know, as well as you will later, the blessings which have here been yours. It is a beautiful sight to see children in a place like The Child City, slowly growing into manhood and womanhood. I think it is a beautiful sight to see your hands and brains trained for service. I trust that your training here has come to you in order that you may carry the standard of The Child City with you wherever you go."

"I believe the finest things you have learned here is the love of work. When you go out into the world, you will find that one of the chief advantages will be that in The Child City you have learned how to work. Here we have tried to train not only your hand and your brain, but your heart as well. Young America is a lesson of unselfish devotion to the ideal viewpoint that every child is entitled to enjoy the privileges of a democratic form of government . . . that every child is entitled to at least a high school education and a trade."

"My personal good wishes go with each of you. I know you will be successful in whatever you do. My blessing to you."

Everything became final. My eyes were very blurry. The orchestra started playing the recessional and we went down the steps, my mother was waiting for me; she hugged me.

We had just about enough time to go to the halls, get lunch and report immediately to the band room to dress in our uniforms.

Even though I had done this parade on the football field every Sunday, this performance was the last I would participate in. The audience attendance was reported to be about 10,000 people.

When we returned to the far end of the field and were at-ease, my band director walked up and down the ranks talking to us grads. He squeezed my arm with his hand and with the other arm he hugged me around the shoulder. I almost dropped my horn. I hugged him, my whole heart seeming to flood into my eyes. Like so many other kids, we had gone through The Child City adopting adults as our fathers. I was leaving the strongest father image I had ever had.

How much of me was wrapped in this relationship was not to emerge until years later. There wasn't a day when I was absent from his influence. He was with me at the contest, rejoiced in my honors, and encouraged me to aspire, to know I was a winner in more than music. He led me without opening doors but showed me how to open them for myself. He spared me few disciplinary measures but made certain I knew the discipline of practice, of performing, of responsibility to myself if I were to achieve. The model to emulate was within him; he could be no different.

He seemed to know intuitively how to motivate, his standards were unwavering. I matched them and flourished in the joy that comes from knowing I did my very best. I gave of myself and received more than the giving.

The cannon went off, and as the flag lowered we played the Star Spangled Banner. As I watched his baton, it was as if he was waving goodbye, yet, assuring me all would be well.

The exhilaration of graduation day was enough to keep other thoughts out of my mind. I returned to my room on the third floor of New York Hall; tired, filled with the wonder of now being graduated. I undressed, hung up my clothes in my usual habitual manner and at the same moment, I realized this would be the last night I would be in this room. As I had no roommate, I was doubly impressed with the aloneness of the moment. This was the last time I would put my clothes on hangers, the last time I would pull the metal drawer open from my dresser, the last time I would hear the creaking springs from my single size bed.

The moonlight reflected on the floor and framed the window. I sat on the wooden box that covered the heating pipes that circled from room to room. It was always my favorite place; a place I could sit, lean my head against the wall and just look out into the night. I sat a long time staring at the water tower reaching to the sky, the smoke from the steam whistle circling upward, waiting for the pull of the wire to shout its greeting to the entire campus.

The water tower loomed like a giant erector set, so familiar, so much a part of my life. It was the first impression I had of Mooseheart when I entered eleven years ago. Everything I looked at ouside the window framed a life I lived and loved and surprisingly tied my life together in a tight knot. I saw the auditorium, the industrial building, the laundry, all floating in front of me. Tears blurred the vision of a life I would no longer enjoy.

This was my 'last night' in this room; my last night at Mooseheart; my last night, the last of all nights I would be living here. I had not cried since I first came to Mooseheart. Strangely, it was in this same hall that I cried when I felt the loneliness of arrival so many years ago.

The inner pain of happy memories and feeling their loss was evident in the soaked pillow the next morning. I lay silent, staring at the ceiling, my dresser mirror reflecting the sun and igniting its glow from the walls. Such a small space, my room, but everything it contained within was me. When I leave it today, would I take me with me, or would I be lost to me? I had all questions, the fears, and the anxieties that not knowing how I would be me without Mooseheart. How do I leave when I want to stay?

I had no choice. My suitcase lay open on the floor and I was the one to pack it. Into it I lay my new graduation suit, worn only once yesterday. I had five shirts, two pants, shorts, socks, my 'everyday shoes'.

I stuffed a few books and odds and ends from my dresser top, and stuff that I loved for some reason and could not leave. The snap to the suitcase jarred my brain in the realization that everything I owned was contained in this oblong box. The $200.00 I was given by the school to 'help me get settled' was neatly tucked into a new wallet, something I had never possessed in my entire life. I knew little of the value of money or spending so I found I had no security in it.

I stood a long time in my doorway, looking back into the precious moments that were my life in this room. As I descended the stairway, I was momentarily thrown back into the memory of a room on the second floor where I spent my first day at Mooseheart. I had tears when I left my room a few minutes ago but now burst into a full, blasting bawl. I was soon joined by other guys; lugging their suitcases, and all slobbering over the stairway to the first floor.

Breakfast was tasteless. The memories that we gulped were nurturing and served to help us walk the long sidewalk to the curb where we entered the bus that would take us to Aurora and the train station.

I don't remember the ride for I was too involved in feelings and emotions, all tugging and yanking from my gut; the physical, mental, emotional and spiritual part of me that was me. As we passed the Arboretum, memories flooded my mind of grandpa's car, full of five boys, their mother and an aunt entering a strange place of which we knew nothing. Now we were leaving, with everything in a packed suitcase.

I don't remember much of Aurora and the train, how I got on, or the ride to Chicago. I could not get myself out of Mooseheart.

Reflections

As I read through life within these pages, I reflected upon certain aspects of extreme importance and value. Discipline is important; it gives a freedom to use the most demanding creative elements of the human spirit. Growing up means getting bumps in your life, bruises to your ego, cuts in your relationships. We are self-healers.

It is good to give yourself to another, to be appreciative, to trust those whom you value and emulate.

There should be time by oneself, with oneself, for oneself.

There is more introspection if one can share with nature in its natural state.

It's important that one become immersed in one of the arts, not just crafts, but also a skill that demands of himself, that he must nurture of himself, that cannot just be given to him; he must earn it the hard way.

There is a life-long pleasure in working, doing. The dignity of living is inevitably wrapped in it.

There should not always be a choice. Strength is often achieved by knowing there is no other way.

Loving means loving yourself.

Giving means giving of yourself.

Sometimes denial is the greatest love you can give to yourself or someone else.

Learn to express yourself through a talent, your gift, and life will be happy for you.

If you are a man, be loving. If you are a woman, be lovingly lovely.

Believe in a Supreme Being.

Respect effort as much as results.

You will be loved for what you are.

It takes your whole life to grow up, you will go through cycles but the germ is within your soul, the cycles will not be complete until death.

Life is growing up to the most fulfilling you can be.

Open yourself to others; you are more alike than different.

Don't be afraid to fail, you can only succeed.

The raising of children is the most important job in the world.

Love your children for someone else to love.

Seek new ways in all things; you are infinity in your soul.

Believe your life is blessed and you will be loved.

Read the lives of great people and great achievements.

*Read the lives of life and you will find yourself
a hundred times.*

Mediocrity is the curse of all arts.

Forgive yourself; forgive others.

Know there is a knowing and you have a profound faith.

Printed in the USA
CPSIA information can be obtained
at www.ICGtesting.com
LVHW041236051023
760079LV00002B/529

9 781939 288202